WEEKENDS FOR TWO IN THE SOUTHWEST

Weekends for Two in the SOUTHWEST

50 Romantic Getaways

BILL GLEESON

PHOTOGRAPHS BY CARY HAZLEGROVE

CHRONICLE BOOKS

SAN FRANCISCO

Contents

Acknowledgments

The author and photographer wish to thank the following people for their assistance, inspiration, and support.

Yvonne Gleeson, research assistance
Bob and Ferne Gleeson
Richard and Isabel Gomes
Lucy Hazlegrove
Sam Randall
Valerie Shaff
Glenn Reinke
Anne Butler
Carolyn Walker

Text copyright © 1997 by Bill Gleeson
Photographs copyright © 1997 by Cary Hazlegrove
Book Design by Robin Weiss.

Library of Congress Cataloging-in-Publication Data available.

ISBN 0-8118-0884-X

Printed in Hong Kong.

Distributed in Canada by Raincoast Books
8680 Cambie Street
Vancouver, B.C. V6P 6M9

10 9 8 7 6 5 4 3 2 1

Chronicle Books
85 Second Street
San Francisco, CA 94105

Introduction

Before you buy a car, you take a test drive. Before you select a tomato, you give it a squeeze. Before you purchase a skirt, you try it on. But how do you go about choosing a romantic getaway destination?

If you were Goldilocks, you could make a bed-to-bed comparison. But if you live in New York —or Phoenix for that matter—and you're planning a trip to Sedona, dropping by for a preview probably isn't in the cards. Instead, you're more apt to take a recommendation from well-intended, but not necessarily romantically enlightened, friends. You might base your decision on a self-serving or even misleading brochure, or use a thick auto club guide with a three-line description and no photos.

It's a process that's about as predictable as throwing dice. Sometimes you win; sometimes you lose.

Picking a winning destination brings relaxation and coziness, which helps set the stage for romance. On the other hand, making the wrong choice can be as romantically rewarding as taking a long cold shower alone.

In choosing fifty romantic places from a lengthy list of outstanding Southwest properties, we have provided our readers with a range of accommodations in terms of rates, size, location, ambience, and setting. Our selections vary from small, inexpensive bed-and-breakfast inns to pricey, full-service luxury resorts. Settings range from remote desert oases and small villages to thriving city centers and high mountain hideaways.

Rooms for Romance

When evaluating the romantic appeal of inns, hotels, and resorts for the *Weekends for Two* series, we consider the following criteria, honed through visits to hundreds of destinations. In the Southwest, our romantic checklist included:

- Private bathrooms (a must in our opinion; we'll tell you if any are shared)
- In-room fireplaces or kivas
- Tubs or showers designed for two
- Breakfast in bed
- Feather beds and cushy comforters
- Canopied, four-poster, king-sized beds
- Couches, love seats, bancos, or nooks for sitting together
- Private decks, patios, or balconies with inspirational views
- Enchanting Southwestern decor and special touches such as fresh flowers and music
- Rooms where smoking is not permitted

Few destinations featured in this book offer a complete menu of such niceties, but each offers at least some.

We also sought out places that exude that overall, sometimes difficult-to-describe intimate atmosphere that engenders romance, as well as those providing pleasant service and respect for privacy.

Finally, we avoided destinations referred to in the lodging industry as "homestays." These are private homes in which a room or rooms are rented out to travelers, often by owners lacking skill in the art of innkeeping.

During our visits to each destination, we discovered special rooms that are particularly conducive to a romantic experience, and we've devoted a good part of this book to details of particularly romantic rooms and suites. When booking your getaway reservation, don't hesitate to ask about the availability of a specific room—especially if you already have a personal favorite.

Tables for Two

At the beginning of each section, we've identified particularly noteworthy restaurants near our featured destinations. These were sampled by us and/or recommended by innkeepers whose opinions we respect. Keep in mind, however, that restaurants—and chefs—come and go. Accordingly, we suggest you balance these recommendations with updates and new choices offered by your innkeeper. He or she will be happy to offer suggestions.

A Word About Rates

Travelers scouting Southwest highways for discount lodgings can still find a no-frills motel room for $50, but this guide isn't for bargain hunters. We were pleasantly surprised by the number of very reasonably priced lodgings discovered during our travels, but many of the special rooms we describe carry rates that are more than $150 per night.

To help you plan your getaway budget, approximate 1996 rates for specific rooms are noted within each description. Keep in mind that an increasing number of establishments require two-night minimum stays on weekends and holidays, so plan your budget accordingly.

In the Southwest, rates frequently vary with seasons, with the high season (or in season) commanding the steepest tariffs. Keep in mind, however, that the high season varies from climate to climate and inn to inn. In hotter locales like Tuscon, high season could be October through April, while in temperate Sedona, the high season usually runs from March through mid-November. In Santa Fe and Taos, whose comparatively cool summers attract travelers from the simmering lowlands, high season generally runs from May through October. Bargains are often available during low season (or off season).

High-season rates per couple are classified at the end of each listing in the following ranges, not including tax:

> Moderate: Under $150
> Expensive: $150-$200
> Deluxe: Over $200

Final Notes

No payment was sought or accepted from any establishment in exchange for a listing in this book.

Food, wine, and flowers were occasionally added to our photo scenes for styling purposes. Some inns provide these amenities; others do not. Please ask when making a reservation whether these items are complimentary or whether they're provided for an extra charge.

Also, please understand that we cannot guarantee that these properties will maintain furnishings or standards as they existed on our visit, and we very much appreciate hearing from readers if their experience is at variance with our descriptions. Reader comments are carefully consulted in the creation and revision of each *Weekends for Two* volume. Your opinions are critical.

SOUTHERN ARIZONA

Daytime Diversions

Valley of the Sun shoppers head for the Borgata, Biltmore Fashion Park, and Scottsdale Fashion Square, among many others. Tower Plaza Mall holds the only ice-skating rink in Phoenix, and there's a huge IMAX theater in the Scottsdale Galleria.

The Phoenix Zoo, open daily, is home to more than one thousand critters, while the Desert Botanical Garden in Papago Park boasts more than ten thousand cacti. Ask your innkeeper about Phoenix-area horseback rides.

On the outskirts of Tucson, Saguaro National Monument is home to hundreds of thousands of the multi-armed sentinels, which are native only to the Sonoran Desert. A tram system transports day-trippers into Sabino Canyon, famous for its waterfalls and natural pools.

There are extensive collections of pre-Columbian and Western art at the Tucson Museum of Art. Also in Tucson, the Arizona-Sonora Desert Museum is considered one of the world's finest showcases of natural wonders.

Visitors to mile-high Bisbee will want to browse the town's antique shops, art galleries, and gift shops. You can even explore an inactive copper mine. Excursions from Bisbee include Tombstone, Cochise Stronghold, and Ramsey Canyon Preserve.

Tables for Two

Touche Ole, 37 Main Street, Bisbee
Cafe Roka, 45 Main Street, Bisbee
8700 (at the Citadel), 8700 East Pinnacle Peak Road, Scottsdale
Mancuelo's of Scottsdale, The Borgata, Scottsdale
Christopher's, 2398 East Camelback Road, Phoenix
Bavarian Point, 4815 East Main Street, Mesa
The American Grill, 1233 East Alma School Road, Mesa
The Tack Room, 2800 North Sabino Canyon Road, Tucson
Charles Restaurant, 6400 East El Dorado Circle, Tucson

The Greenway House

401 Cole Avenue
Bisbee, AZ 85603
Telephone toll free: (800) 253-3325

Eight rooms, each with private bath. Complimentary
continental breakfast served in your room. Handicapped access. Smoking is not permitted. Two-night
minimum stay required during weekends and holiday
periods. Moderate.

Getting There
From Interstate 10, drive south on Highway 80 through
Tombstone to Bisbee, past Old Bisbee to the traffic
circle. Turn right on Bisbee Road and right on Cole
Avenue, and follow to inn.

Its location within a heavily mined area just outside of Bisbee may not be the garden spot of the Southwest, but this incongruously placed Craftsman-style mansion is one of the most handsome Arizona bed-and-breakfast inns we've discovered.

Not surprisingly, the turn-of-the-century home was built by a local mining company executive. The residence was among the area's most lavish, and the detailing, like pressed copper ceilings and stenciling, has been lovingly restored and preserved. There's even a tiny old elevator that

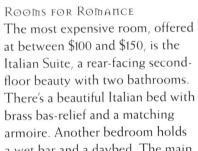

operates between the first and second floors.

A spacious game room downstairs holds a fine pool table and shuffleboard, and all guest rooms have televisions and videocassette players.

ROOMS FOR ROMANCE

The most expensive room, offered at between $100 and $150, is the Italian Suite, a rear-facing second-floor beauty with two bathrooms. There's a beautiful Italian bed with brass bas-relief and a matching armoire. Another bedroom holds a wet bar and a daybed. The main bathroom is tiled and holds a large clawfoot tub.

A hand-carved king-sized bed is the centerpiece of the Victorian Suite (around $100), a rear-corner room that's also furnished with an antique settee, a huge armoire, and a small kitchen with a table and chairs. The bathroom has a small clawfoot-tub-and-shower combination.

The Wicker Room, appointed with a wicker love seat, has a queen-sized brass and iron bed covered with a wedding ring quilt. A kitchenette is hidden behind closet doors. In the bathroom is a large clawfoot tub that just might hold two.

The adjacent Carriage House has two large suites. The Southwest Suite (low to mid $100 range) on the first floor is an apartment-sized unit with a living room, a dining room, a kitchen, and a large bedroom.

Travelers should be aware that while the Greenway House has a Bisbee mailing address, it's located in the neighboring community of Warren. Bisbee shops and restaurants are about a five-minute drive away.

BISBEE GRAND HOTEL
57 Main Street
Bisbee, AZ 85603
Telephone: (520) 432-5900

Eleven rooms, all with private baths. Complimentary full breakfast served at tables for two. Old West saloon. No handicapped access. Smoking is not permitted. Two-night minimum stay required during holiday periods. Moderate.

Getting There
From Interstate 10, drive south on Highway 80 through Tombstone to Bisbee. The hotel is on Main Street in downtown.

BISBEE GRAND HOTEL ✧ *Bisbee*

We've all seen at least one Western movie in which a lady in red and a grizzled cowboy kick up their heels in a smoky saloon and later disappear together up a darkened stairway. Today's visitors to the Bisbee Grand Hotel are a bit more refined than the rough-and-tumble folk depicted on the silver screen, but this relic is right out of a Western movie set.

A book encompassing a large portion of the fabled Old West wouldn't be complete without an authentic hostelry representative of that bygone era. We've not discovered a better romantic time machine than the Bisbee Grand.

Guests get their first taste of old Bisbee when checking in at a restored century-old saloon on the hotel's ground floor. Some of the fixtures here were once owned by legendary Tombstone lawman Wyatt Earp. Your room key will unlock the door to a stairway leading to the hotel's collection of second-floor guest rooms.

ROOMS FOR ROMANCE

For romantic getaways, we suggest three suites, which are generously sized and have their own bathrooms. Two rooms have private baths down the hall.

The Victorian Suite (low $100 range) is one of two sensuous front-facing suites. Sporting a blushingly bawdy decor, the suite is decorated with a canopy bed draped in flowing red fabric. French doors separate the bedroom from a sitting room containing a tiny antique love seat and a tiled decorative fireplace.

Next door is the Oriental Suite (around $100), a lovers' lair appointed with an ornate king-sized Chinese teak wedding bed. It's one of the most appealing beds we've found in our Southwest travels. The suite's sitting room holds a couch and a decorative fireplace.

The Garden Suite (around $100) is carpeted in deep red and equipped with an antique queen-sized bed. The sitting room has a decorative fireplace, an antique couch, and a huge mirror.

The Peppertrees
Bed and Breakfast Inn

724 East University Boulevard
Tucson, AZ 85719
Telephone: (520) 622-7167; toll-free: (800) 348-5763

Five rooms, each with private bath. Complimentary
full gourmet breakfast served at communal table and
tables for two. No handicapped access. Smoking is
not permitted. Two-night minimum stay required
during holiday periods. Moderate.

Getting There
From Interstate 10 in Tucson, take the Speedway
exit and drive east to Euclid Avenue. Turn right and
follow to University Boulevard. Turn right; inn is
on the left.

THE PEPPERTREES
BED AND BREAKFAST INN ❖ *Tucson*

There's something about a college town that stirs our romantic souls. Maybe it's that the ever-present examples of young love remind us of our own youthful college days of passions and dreams.

We rediscovered that energizing spirit on the campus of the University of Arizona, and followed it down the street to the Peppertrees. You don't have to be a student to savor this delightful inn, which shares a downtown neighborhood with sorority and fraternity houses.

Two California pepper trees frame this quaint turn-of-the-century home, which now holds three comfortable guest rooms. Two other rooms are contained in a rear guest house. On the pretty flower-filled courtyard that separates the two buildings, many college romances blossom each year into wedding ceremonies.

Guests have easy access to the university campus and to Tucson's Fourth Avenue shopping district, either by foot or by a renovated trolley, which rolls along University Boulevard in front of the inn.

ROOMS FOR ROMANCE
Our favorites are the two rooms in the guest house at the rear of the property. Sunset (mid $100 range) has a living room with a television and a couch, a full kitchen, and a small private patio reached by French doors. Upstairs are two bedrooms, one with a queen-sized bed, and a small bathroom with a tub-and-shower combination. The adjacent Sunrise suite has a similar floor plan.

In the 730 annex, Phoebe's Room (under $100) has a king-sized bed, 1930s furnishings, and a private bathroom with a shower stall. It shares the main house living room with the Jenny Room, a front-facing corner room.

In the main house, Penelope (under $100) is a lovely room with five windows and a cushioned church pew, but the private bathroom is located across the hall.

THE SUN CATCHER
105 North Avenida Javelina
Tucson, AZ 85748
Telephone: (520) 885-0883

Four rooms, each with private bath. Complimentary full
breakfast served at communal table. Complimentary
refreshments. Swimming pool and health club privileges.
Handicapped access. Smoking is not permitted. Two-
night minimum stay required during weekends and
holiday periods. Moderate to expensive.

Getting There
From Interstate 10 in Tucson, take the Broadway exit and
drive east on Broadway for thirteen miles. Two and a half
miles past the Houghton Road intersection (and past a
"dead end" sign), turn left on Avenida Javelina and drive
to inn on left.

THE SUN CATCHER ✤ *Tucson*

In our romantically biased opinion, those who limit their Tucson visit to the downtown area are missing the best part. It's not until shopping centers are replaced by the wide open Sonoran Desert and traffic lights give way to twisted saguaro that you feel the region's true magical potential.

Driving for miles away from the city toward Saguaro National Monument, we feared more than once that we'd overshot our mark. Then, just yards before Broadway dead-ended at the base of the formidable Rincon Ridge, we caught sight of the remote road that would lead us to one of southern Arizona's most romantic inns.

The architecturally stunning home is set on four unspoiled acres that showcase the desert's awesome beauty. Two rugged mountain ranges loom in the distance.

Guest rooms each contain fresh flowers, a writing desk, a television and videocassette player (there are more than two hundred movies to choose from), a telephone, hair dryers, bathrobes, and upscale toiletries. In addition to the on-site swimming pool, access to Tucson tennis and health clubs is offered to guests free of charge. Complimentary refreshments are available around the clock.

ROOMS FOR ROMANCE

You'll not be disappointed with any of the four bedrooms, each named after and reflecting the particular decor of an internationally famous hotel. Each is priced in the mid $100 range.

Named for the Oriental Hotel of Bangkok, the Oriental Room is the inn's premiere romantic accommodation. This front-facing room is decorated with Oriental art and features a huge marble-floored bathroom with a spa tub for two, a separate shower, and a bidet.

Also often requested by honeymooners is the Connaught Room, appointed with mahogany Chippendale furnishings. The queen-sized bed is covered with a Battenburg lace comforter.

The brick fireplace is perfect for chilly desert evenings. The bathroom holds a large tub-and-shower combination.

The inn's only canopied bed is found in the Four Seasons Room, where a built-in bookcase is stocked with books on Queen Elizabeth I. The bathroom has a tub-and-shower combination, and French doors open onto the pool deck.

The Regent Room has a contemporary Oriental look and is furnished with several intriguing items, including a Tibetan prayer rug. There's an oversized shower with a tiled bench in the bathroom.

The Lodge at Ventana Canyon

6200 North Clubhouse Lane
Tucson, AZ 85715
Telephone: (520) 577-1400; toll-free: (800) 828-5701

Forty-nine suites, each with private bath, kitchen, and oversized tub. Restaurants, lounge, two eighteen-hole golf courses, driving range, twelve tennis courts, swimming pool, and exercise rooms. Handicapped access. Smoking is allowed. No minimum stay requirement. Deluxe.

Getting There

From Interstate 10 in Tucson, exit at Ina Road and drive east to Skyline. Turn right on Skyline (which becomes Sunrise), and follow to Kolb Road. Turn left on Kolb and drive a half mile to the Ventana Canyon Golf and Racquet Club gatehouse on right.

The Lodge at Ventana Canyon ❖ *Tucson*

W ould you prefer experiencing the magnificent Sonoran Desert from a couch in your private air-conditioned living room, from a refreshing pool, from a hiking path, or from a lush fairway lined with saguaro cacti? If your answer is "all of the above," you'll likely enjoy this resort as much as we did.

Our personal favorite Southwest desert destination, The Lodge at Ventana Canyon is the quintessence of the all-in-one luxury resort, providing a generous range of activities, from recreation to romance.

Overlooking Tucson from the foothills of the Santa Catalina Mountains, Ventana Canyon entices travelers with not one, but two eighteen-hole PGA golf courses, a huge swimming pool, and a dozen lighted tennis courts. There are also fully equipped exercise rooms and two restaurants.

Rooms for Romance

Completely renovated and refurbished in 1995, the resort's forty-nine one- and two-bedroom suites each have a kitchen stocked daily with complimentary refreshments, a separate living room with cushy furnishings, multiple televisions and telephones, a spacious and well-equipped bathroom with an oversized tub, and a private balcony or patio with views of the Santa Catalina Mountains or the city of Tucson. Keep in mind that rates noted below drop substantially during the summer months; high season is usually mid-January through mid-April.

Suite 229 (around $300) is the one most often requested by honeymooners and romantics in the know. Boasting approximately nine hundred square feet, it has a king-sized bed and overlooks a fairway and the distant mountains.

One way to soften the high-season tariff would be to visit with another couple and share the cost of a two-bedroom suite (around $400 total). For example, Suite 221, our apartment-sized two-bedroom unit, was equipped with a kitchenette, a spacious living room, a master bedroom, a loft bedroom reached by a circular stairway, and two well-equipped bathrooms. One of these held a deep soaking tub-and-shower combination.

Arizona Inn
2200 East Elm Street
Tucson, AZ 85719
Telephone: (520) 325-1541; toll-free: (800) 933-1093

Eighty-three rooms and suites, each with private bath;
thirteen with fireplaces. Swimming pool, tennis
courts, two restaurants, and lounge. Handicapped
access. Smoking is allowed. No minimum stay
requirement. Moderate to deluxe.

Getting There
From Interstate 10 in Tucson, exit on Speedway
Boulevard and drive east on Speedway to Campbell
Avenue. Turn left and drive a half mile to Elm Street.
Turn right and follow a half mile to inn on right.

As the story goes, Isabella Greenway, who built the Arizona Inn in the early 1930s, was a stickler for detail. Some still remember her wandering the construction site with a pillow, assuming recumbent positions to make firsthand judgments about where to place a window for just the right view from bed.

That fine-tuned attention to comfort is still embraced by Isabella's family members, who have carefully preserved and nurtured this fabled grande dame of southern Arizona resorts for more than half a century.

A lush retreat in the midst of busy Tucson, Arizona Inn occupies fourteen colorful acres of mature trees, gardens, and lawns. Its clientele ranges from families to businesspeople, not to mention the many couples who find this timeless resort an inspiring year-round romantic getaway destination.

The inn has a reputation as a retreat for well-heeled travelers, and well-to-do locals as well as celebrities are drawn to its highly rated restaurant. However, prices here are refreshingly affordable; at the time of our visit, they started at under $100.

Rooms for Romance

The inn's comfortable and spacious guest rooms are spread among a half dozen or so pueblo-style stucco buildings. A number of rooms have private patios. Furnishings, many of which are as old as the inn, are traditional. Bathrooms boast contemporary appointments.

Rooms 250, 251 (our home for a night), 252, and 187 are recommended, with a caveat: they are located on a side street and do not offer convenient access to the swimming pool and tennis courts. You'll have to walk right through the main lobby or a dark working area to get there. We found rooms 178 and 186, although also very private, to be inconveniently situated as well.

We prefer those rooms situated within the main compound facing the nicely sculpted and colorful interior lawn and garden area.

GOLD CANYON RANCH
6100 South Kings Ranch Road
Apache Junction, AZ 85219
Telephone toll-free: (800) 624-6445

Fifty-seven rooms, each with private bath and indoor or outdoor fireplace; half with tubs or spas for two. Golf course, tennis courts, swimming pool, restaurant, and lounge. Handicapped access. Smoking is allowed. No minimum stay requirement. Expensive to deluxe.

Getting There
From Phoenix, drive east on Highway 60 (Superstition Freeway). Follow the two-lane portion of Highway 60 for four miles and turn left on Kings Ranch Road. Drive one mile to resort on left. The resort is approximately forty minutes from Sky Harbor Airport.

GOLD CANYON RANCH ✣ *Apache Junction*

Forget the legendary "Lost Dutchman's Mine" purportedly hidden in the adjacent Superstition Mountains. Gold Canyon Ranch is the X mark on our Arizona treasure map.

This desert golf resort, so close, yet so far from the fast pace of Phoenix, is a favorite of metropolitan-area couples in the know looking for a convenient romantic getaway. The stunning, whitewashed, Spanish-style *casitas* are set against craggy hills, from which the city's distant shimmering lights can be seen at night.

Also worthy of note are the resort's impeccably tended grounds, which are profuse with mesquite and several types of cacti, including aging saguaro, spiny strawberry, Arizona barrel, and prickly pear.

ROOMS FOR ROMANCE

We found some of the decor, like the metal kitchenette cabinetry in our room, to be a bit dated, but Gold Canyon Ranch's *casitas* are some of the Phoenix area's most romantically equipped. All have woodburning fireplaces, and nearly half of the accommodations come with private indoor or outdoor tubs or spas for two. The generous-sized rooms, the smallest of which are nearly five hundred square feet, also have either a kitchenette or a wet bar.

As if our Gold Canyon Resort *casita* (Room 108) didn't offer enough romantic potential, our visit coincided with Valentine's Day. Toasting the end of the day from our indoor spa in front of a flickering fire, we were easy prey for Cupid.

For romantic getaways, we give our highest recommendation to the rooms with the spacious private spas (low $200 range), all of which have private patios. Rooms with indoor spas have two queen-sized beds and private patios, while those with indoor whirlpool bathtubs have one king-sized bed. Those with outdoor spas have either two queens or one king-sized bed.

Standard rooms (mid $100 range) are not equipped with private spas, but have outdoor patio fireplaces.

Guests should be advised that some of the tantalizing outdoor spas are visible from adjacent walkways, so swimsuits are de rigueur. However, Rooms 429 and 104 offer patio spas that are completely private, and Room 29 boasts a great city light view. Unfortunately, the availability of these rooms can't be guaranteed.

Rates noted above are for the resort's high season, from January through mid-May. Summer rates for spa rooms are in the mid $100 range.

Maricopa Manor
Bed & Breakfast Inn
15 West Pasadena Avenue
Phoenix, AZ 85013
Telephone: (602) 274-6302

Five rooms, each with private bath, television,
and telephone. Complimentary continental
breakfast served in your room. Swimming pool.
No handicapped access. Smoking is not permitted.
No minimum stay required. Moderate.

Getting There
From Interstate 17, take the Camelback exit and
drive east on Camelback Road. Turn left on Third
Avenue and drive one block to Pasadena Avenue.
Turn right and follow to inn.

Maricopa Manor
Bed & Breakfast Inn ❖ *Phoenix*

Maricopa Manor is perhaps Phoenix's most romantic downtown B&B, but guests here are more apt to be seen clutching briefcases than the hand of a loved one. During the work week, that is.

On Friday afternoons, after discerning businessfolk have departed this centrally located inn for parts unknown, happy, casually dressed couples begin arriving, ready for a romantic weekend in a city that's literally at their feet.

When constructed in the 1920s, this handsome Spanish-style home enjoyed a rural setting a few miles from the center of town. As the city has spread over the years, Maricopa Manor has found itself literally in the shadow of bustling Phoenix, at the edge of a mature, comfortable neighborhood.

Although the pulse of the city beats nearby, the Maricopa Manor estate remains an Eden of sorts, boasting lovely trees, lush lawns, a swimming pool, and inviting nooks for outdoor relaxing.

Rooms for Romance

Once home to a family of a dozen children, the grand manor could easily have been chopped into as many tiny bedrooms. Thankfully, the inn has been held to a manageable five suites, so guests aren't likely to feel crowded. All rooms are offered in the low $100 range.

The most popular among visiting romantics is the Library Suite, whose centerpiece is a king-sized bed with a rich blue canopy. This room also offers a love seat, a full-sized desk, and a private entry off an outdoor deck.

Once a small, self-contained home, Palo Verde is a nice two-bedroom suite furnished with a Franklin stove, a king-sized bed, a wicker love seat, and a small, sunny dining alcove furnished with a table and chairs.

The inn's separate guest house consists of two suites: Reflections Past and Reflections Future. The former suite has a living room with a fireplace and walls of antique mirrors. The bedroom holds a king-sized bed with a canopy.

Our favorite room in the inn is the spacious, art deco–style Reflections Future, boldly decorated with brass, glass, and mirrors. This suite, done in black and white, boasts a living room, a sun room, a kitchen, and a breakfast area. The bedroom has a queen-sized bed.

The small Victorian Room, whose private bath is along the hall outside the room, is most often used by visiting business people. We don't recommend this accommodation for romantic getaways.

RENAISSANCE COTTONWOODS RESORT

6160 North Scottsdale Road
Scottsdale, AZ 85253
Telephone: (602) 991-1414

One hundred seventy rooms, each with private bath; 34 with fireplaces; 106 with spa tubs for two. Complimentary morning coffee and newspaper delivered to your room. Two swimming pools, lighted tennis courts, jogging/fitness trail, croquet court, putting green, and restaurant. Handicapped access. Smoking is allowed. Five-night minimum night stay required during high-season periods. Deluxe.

Getting There
From Interstate 10 near Sky Harbor Airport, follow Squaw Peak Parkway (Highway 51) north to Lincoln Drive exit. Turn right and follow Lincoln Drive for approximately seven miles to Scottsdale Road. Turn right on Scottsdale Road to first traffic light. Turn right into resort.

RENAISSANCE COTTONWOODS RESORT ✦ *Scottsdale*

For those who like to shop till they drop, there's no more convenient and romantic place to drop and unwind than this rambling resort complex set right next door to the Borgata, Scottsdale's classy, Italian-style shopping complex. A trolley offers transportation to the Scottsdale Fashion Square and the Biltmore Fashion Park.

The fast pace of Scottsdale may be just steps away, but inside Renaissance Cottonwoods Resort the living is tranquil and easy. Multi-unit structures dot the expansive grounds, connected by a series of tree-shaded walkways. There are more than one hundred fifty rooms here, but accommodations are placed in small clusters so as to ensure a reasonable level of privacy.

ROOMS FOR ROMANCE

There are three types of accommodations at the resort: Tucson Suites (mid $200 range), Phoenix Suites (around $300), and Flagstaff guest rooms (low $200 range).

We chose to include this property because of one particularly romantic feature found within each of the Tucson and Phoenix suites: a spa for two on your own privately enclosed patio under the Arizona sky. Those unable to afford the extra tariff for a spa room still have access to water. The resort boasts a huge swimming pool and a patio that faces Camelback Mountain.

Our two-room Tucson Suite, No. 243, offered a spacious living room facing a small lattice-covered front patio. We enjoyed our breakfast at the patio table after being lulled awake not by a noisy alarm but by softly cooing doves.

The carpeted living room was furnished with a wet bar, cushioned chairs, a sleeper sofa, and a television. The separate bedroom contained two queen-sized beds and another television. The two-person in-ground spa was situated on a completely private walled patio just off the bedroom.

At the top end of the scale, the deluxe Phoenix Suites come with a kitchen, an oversized bathroom, and a woodburning fireplace, as well as more elegant furnishings.

Inn at the Citadel
8700 East Pinnacle Peak Road
Scottsdale, AZ 85255
Telephone: (602) 585-0297

Eleven rooms, each with private bath and deep tub for two; five with fireplaces. Complimentary continental breakfast served in restaurant or in your room. Restaurant. Handicapped access. Smoking is not permitted. Two-night minimum stay required during weekends. Deluxe.

Getting There
From Interstate 10 near Sky Harbor Airport, follow Squaw Peak Parkway (Highway 51) north to Shea Boulevard. Drive east on Shea Boulevard to Pima Road and turn left. Follow Pima Road to Pinnacle Peak Road. The Citadel center is on the northwest corner.

İ ᴨ ᴨ   ᴀᴛ   ᴛʜᴇ   Cİᴛᴀᴅᴇʟ   ✛   *Scottsdale*

An upscale retail and corporate complex is the unlikely setting for one of Arizona's most luxurious small inns. Spread discreetly above and amid boutiques, offices, and restaurants, and identified by minimal signage, the Inn at the Citadel is our most inconspicuous romantic hideaway. We wouldn't be surprised if most shoppers were completely unaware of this Scottsdale jewel.

The eleven rooms and suites are elegant and comfortable, and feature a mix of antique and contemporary furnishings, original art, king-sized beds, and spacious tiled bathrooms with double sinks and deep tubs big enough for two. Five rooms have woodburning fireplaces. Televisions are stowed in armoires.

The rooms are located along a second-floor outdoor walkway reached by an elevator. All except Rooms 1 and 11 have patio areas with tables and chairs. Most overlook a pleasant courtyard and restaurant.

The inn is located several miles from the heart of Scottsdale, and there is no swimming pool on site.

Rooms for Romance

According to the inn's staff, Rooms 9 and 11 are the two rooms best suited for anniversaries, honeymoons, and other special romantic celebrations. Room 9, which has a fireplace, looks toward Pinnacle Peak, while Room 11, with its rounded walls and enchanting bedside fireplace, faces the courtyard.

Room 4 has a sitting area appointed with a fireplace and a grand antique desk. In the separate bedroom is a king-sized bed with a handsome antique headboard and two chairs. Rooms 7 and 8 also have separate sleeping rooms.

The least expensive room, at around $200 per night, is Room 1, equipped with two double beds. All the other rooms carry tariffs in the mid to upper $200 range.

Northern Arizona

Daytime Diversions

At the Grand Canyon's south entrance you'll find an IMAX theater that displays the canyon's wonders on a seven-story screen. Two of the most popular hiking trails, the Bright Angel and the South Kaibab, start near Grand Canyon Village.

Flagstaff visitors might want to check out the Anasazi Indian ruins at the Wupatki National Monument, thirty-five miles north of town. The Snowbowl ski area is located fourteen miles south of Flagstaff.

Discover the natural forces of Sedona through a vortex tour or an Indian petroglyph hike conducted by Earth Wisdom Tours, (520) 282-4714. Those conspicuous pink jeeps you see around the area take visitors on year-round off-road tours of Sedona's Red Rock country and the Coconino National Forest, (800) 873-3662. If you'd prefer to see Sedona from a saddle, call Kachina Stables at (520) 282-7252. Sedona's popular Tlaquepaque Arts and Crafts Village shopping complex is on Highway 179 at the Oak Creek Bridge.

Visitors to Pinetop-Lakeside have access to the White Mountain trail system, whose 180 miles of bike, hiking, and horse trails connect five parks.

Tables for Two

Brix Grill and Wine Bar, 801 South Milton, Flagstaff
Pasto, 19 East Aspen, Flagstaff
Heartline Cafe, 1610 West Highway 89A, Sedona
Shugrue's Hillside Grill, 671 Highway 179, Sedona
Peacock Room at the Hassayampa Hotel, Gurley and Marina Streets, Prescott
Murphy's, Cortez and Willis Streets, Prescott
The Christmas Tree Restaurant, Woodland Road, Lakeside

BARTRAM'S BED AND BREAKFAST
Woodland Lake Road
Lakeside, AZ 85929
Telephone: (520) 367-1408

Five rooms, each with private bath. Complimentary
full breakfast served at communal table. No handicapped access. Smoking is not permitted. Two-night
minimum stay required during holiday periods.
Moderate.

Getting There
From Highway 260 north of Pinetop, turn west
at stoplight on Woodland Road and drive approximately one mile to the T intersection; turn right on
Woodland Lake Road. Follow to end of road, inn is
on the right. Lakeside is approximately 185 miles
from Phoenix and 210 miles from Tucson.

BARTRAM'S
BED AND BREAKFAST ❖ *Lakeside*

Despite the availability of literally thousands of guest rooms in the Pinetop-Lakeside area, securing suitably romantic accommodations can prove difficult, especially to first-time visitors. Lakeside-bound couples who enjoy a country bed-and-breakfast experience and reasonable prices will find this little inn a delight.

An unpretentious ranch-style home set under tall pines at the end of a woodsy road, Bartram's Bed and Breakfast serves up country comfort and peace and quiet in a friendly, informal atmosphere. The inn's setting, a comfortable distance from the beaten path, should be especially appealing to folks who love the White Mountains region but prefer to avoid the touristy congestion.

Innkeeper Petie Bartram, one of the most personable hosts we encountered in the Southwest, entertains guests with a friendly menagerie, which at the time of our visit included a resident pot-bellied pig named Farnsworth and an exotic parrot. In addition, she tempts her guests with little "extras" that might range from a cup of hot cider at the end of a snowy winter day to a bowl of homemade ice cream in the summer.

ROOMS FOR ROMANCE

The inn's five small country-fresh rooms, all with private baths, are charmingly homespun and are offered for around $85, which includes a full breakfast and afternoon snacks.

Windows in the guest rooms are covered with miniblinds and drapes that match the bedspreads. Walls are tastefully papered.

The Peach Room is a suite whose sitting room includes matching white iron day beds. In the Satin Room, an attractive fireplace sits near the foot of the satin-covered bed. A four-poster iron bed and wicker furniture complement the Garden Room.

Sierra Springs Ranch
Sky-Hi Road
Pinetop, AZ 85935
Telephone: (520) 369-3900; toll-free: (800) 247-7590

Eight cabins, each with bath, kitchen, and fireplace.
Smoking is not permitted. No handicapped access.
Two-night minimum stay required during weekends;
three- to four-night minimum during holiday periods.
Expensive.

Getting There
From Highway 260 one mile east of Pinetop, turn
north on Bucksprings Road. Drive a half mile and turn
left on Tomahawk Road, which becomes Sky-Hi Road.
Follow gravel road for two miles to ranch entrance
on right. The ranch is approximately 190 miles from
Phoenix and 185 miles from Tucson.

In assembling each of our *Weekends for Two* volumes, there's at least one romantic discovery that we would have preferred to keep all to ourselves. In the Southwest, Sierra Springs Ranch is that special place.

If you believe that a visit to the Pinetop-Lakeside region necessarily includes motels, traffic, and pizza parlors, a weekend at this remote seventy-six-acre, all-season resort will enrich the two of you with a soul-stirring new perspective.

The ranch consists of a collection of new and restored cabins that sit under ponderosa pines at the edge of a wide meadow, which sparkles with winter snow before turning a luxuriant green. The property also includes private lakes, a fitness center, a sauna, hiking and ski trails, a gazebo, and a tennis court.

The lack of an on-site restaurant might tempt some visitors to venture into town for dinner, but many guests choose to take advantage of the barbeques and cabin kitchens with table service, savoring an intimate home-cooked meal under the pines.

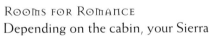

ROOMS FOR ROMANCE
Depending on the cabin, your Sierra Springs Ranch hideaway might feature cedar paneling, pine log walls, an antique clawfoot tub, or a modern shower. Each, however, is richly appointed with comfortable furniture, soft carpeting, and a well-equipped kitchen. All of the rooms listed below are in the mid $100 range.

Romantics will cherish a night or two in the Honeymoon cabin, a nine-hundred-square-foot, one-bedroom charmer with a king-sized bed and a sunny bathroom, where an antique bathtub with a hand-held shower attachment sits in a windowed corner.

The Santa Fe is a similarly sized cabin with two bedrooms. The master bedroom contains a king-sized bed, and the other holds two twins.

The refurbished Barn cottage holds two upstairs bedrooms with two private bathrooms. The Cheyenne and the Pueblo Lodge are the two other multi-bedroom units; these are best suited for large groups but can also accommodate couples at rates in the mid $100 range.

THE MARKS HOUSE
203 East Union Street
Prescott, AZ 86303
Telephone: (520) 778-4632

Four rooms, each with private bath. Complimentary
full breakfast served in dining room. No handicapped
access. Smoking is not permitted. No minimum stay
requirement. Moderate.

Getting There
From Interstate 17, exit at Cordes Junction onto
Highway 69 and follow northwest for thirty-three
miles to Prescott. In Prescott, turn left on Highway
89. Turn left on Marina Street and follow one block
to inn on corner of Marina and Union streets.

Couples looking for a nineteenth-century Arizona experience in a cool, high-altitude locale will enjoy an overnight stay in the Marks House, a fetching downtown home set on a hill just one block from historic Courthouse Square. It's also conveniently close to Prescott shops, galleries, and restaurants.

Built for a prominent Prescott citizen for four thousand dollars just over a century ago, the Queen Anne–style home was crafted from redwood and is festooned with fine oak, maple, and copper finishing. The structure served as a family residence, a boarding house, and a home for the elderly before becoming an inn in the late 1980s.

Owned by actress Beth Maitland, who created the role of Traci Abbott on *The Young and the Restless*, the inn is managed by Beth's friendly parents, Dottie and Harold Viehweg.

Rooms for Romance

The house favorite is the Queen Anne Suite (low $100 range); it occupies half of the second floor and includes the charming turret, which is furnished as a sitting room with a couple of wicker chairs. The bedroom, whose walls are papered in green and white, has a king-sized bed with a wicker headboard. A clawfoot tub sits in a dressing room area adjacent to the bedroom.

Our second favorite room is the front-facing Ivy Suite (low $100 range) on the main floor. This is a two-bedroom chamber that can accommodate two couples.

In Princess Victoria (under $100), a bath house–style copper tub isn't just an antique conversation piece. Set under a row of windows, it's quite functional, offering a great spot for a relaxing bubble bath. However, the toilet is not completely private.

It's the smallest room in the house, but the lacy Tea Rose (under $100) does contain a nice big queen-sized bed. Guests should note that this room's private bath, equipped with a clawfoot tub, is down the hall a few steps.

PLEASANT STREET INN
142 South Pleasant Street
Prescott, AZ 86303
Telephone: (520) 445-4774

Four rooms, each with private bath. Complimentary
full breakfast served at communal table. No handicapped access. Smoking is not permitted. Two-night
minimum stay required during holiday periods.
Moderate.

Getting There
From Interstate 17, exit at Cordes Junction onto
Highway 69 and follow northwest for thirty-three
miles to Prescott. In Prescott, turn left on Highway
89, which becomes Gurley Street. Turn left on
Pleasant Street and follow to inn on right, at the
corner of Pleasant and Goodwin streets.

During a tour of the residential sections of this former Arizona territorial capital city, we made quite a romantic discovery behind the door of a well-tended turn-of-the-century home. Expecting that the vintage exterior would be mirrored inside, we were pleasantly surprised to find a completely updated, enlarged, and very comfortable interior with moderately priced guest rooms.

Moved a block or two in 1990 to its current site on a shady corner of the aptly named Pleasant Street, the old home was adopted by innkeeper Jean Urban, who treats her guests to bright, spacious rooms with rich, traditional furnishings, wall-to-wall carpeting, ceiling fans, and private bathrooms.

Outside, an inviting front deck is arranged with cozy wicker furnishings, providing guests with a quiet place to relax after the three-block walk from Prescott's historic Courthouse Square and downtown shops.

ROOMS FOR ROMANCE

Our highest recommendation is given to the Pine View Suite (low $100 range), an elegant two-room accommodation on the second floor. A comfortable bay-windowed sitting room boasts a pretty, blue-tiled woodburning fireplace and a sofa, and the adjacent bedroom holds a king-sized bed. The bright bathroom has double sinks.

Our other romantic favorite is the Terrace Suite (low $100 range), the only guest room on the first floor. It consists of a separate sitting room with a couch and a chair and a windowless bedroom with a queen-sized bed. The small bathroom holds a tub-and-shower combination.

Offered at the time of our visit for just under $100 per night, the second-floor Garden Room faces the front of the property and is appointed with wicker furnishings and a queen-sized bed. The small bathroom has a tiny sink and a shower stall.

Coventry (under $100) is another second-floor corner room offering a king-sized bed (or two twins) and views of the distant mountains. Traveling romantics should note that this room's spacious and private bath is across the hall.

Canyon Villa Bed and Breakfast

125 Canyon Circle Drive

Sedona, AZ 86351

Telephone: (520) 284-1226; toll-free: (800) 453-1166

Eleven rooms, each with private bath; four with fireplaces. Complimentary full breakfast served at communal tables. Swimming pool. Handicapped access. Smoking is not permitted. Two-night minimum stay required during weekends; three-night minimum during holiday periods. Moderate to expensive.

Getting There

From Interstate 17 (two hours from Phoenix), exit at Highway 179 and drive north for 8.4 miles. Turn left on Bell Rock Boulevard and right on Canyon Circle Drive. Follow to inn on right. The inn is about six miles south of Sedona.

Canyon Villa Bed and Breakfast ❖ *Sedona*

Long after we had departed Sedona, the surreal view from Canyon Villa's Spanish Bayonet Room lingered in our memory. Not only does this entrancing room overlook majestic Bell Rock, a dramatic sandstone landmark, the view, as well as an in-room fireplace, can be savored through French doors from the in-room whirlpool tub as well as from the cozy king-sized bed.

And don't despair if Spanish Bayonet is booked during your visit to Sedona. There are other similarly sumptuous accommodations at this romantic hideaway tucked into a residential area in the Village of Oak Creek, a short drive from Sedona proper.

Even those who are not usually attracted to lobbies and living rooms during a romantic weekend away will be drawn to Canyon Villa's common area, with its high ceilings and hanging fans and a big see-through fireplace. There's a small library with white oak floors, and an expanse of windows overlooks the swimming pool. An outdoor fireplace stands next to the pool, and Bell Rock and Courthouse Butte loom dramatically in the distance.

Rooms for Romance

Spanish Bayonet (low $200 range) is one of five romantic rooms on the inn's second floor. Another favorite here is Strawberry Cactus (upper $100 range), a corner room with vivid blue carpeting, a king-sized bed, and a small balcony with a great regional view. The bathroom holds a whirlpool tub/shower combination.

The other second-floor room with a fireplace, Ocotillo (low $200 range), features Southwestern decor and a king-sized bed.

The two best rooms on the ground floor are the Western-themed Mariposa Room and the king-bedded Claret Cup (around $200), which is more traditionally styled. These rooms have private patios, gas fireplaces, and single-sized whirlpool tubs; Mariposa also has a separate shower.

The Prickly Pear Room (low $100 range), which features a walled patio, is very private, but it lacks the dramatic views of the other rooms. This is the only room without a whirlpool tub.

The Graham Bed & Breakfast Inn
150 Canyon Circle Drive
Sedona, AZ 86351
Telephone: (520) 284-1425

Six rooms, each with private bath and television with videocassette player; four have fireplaces; three have spa tubs for two. Complimentary full breakfast served at communal table, at tables for two, or in your room. Swimming pool and free rental bikes. No handicapped access. Smoking is not permitted. Two-night minimum stay required during weekends; three-night minimum during some holiday periods. Moderate to deluxe.

Getting There
From Interstate 17 (two hours from Phoenix), exit at Highway 179 and drive north for 8.4 miles. Turn left on Bell Rock Boulevard and follow two blocks to inn on right. The inn is about six miles south of Sedona.

THE GRAHAM
BED & BREAKFAST INN ❖ *Sedona*

In our initial planning for this romantic guide to the Southwest, we envisioned one, maybe two, destinations in Sedona. As we toured the area, however, each bend in the road revealed a new and enticing panorama, and each of the inns we visited offered an inviting experience.

Located a few miles south of Sedona in the Village of Oak Creek, The Graham Bed & Breakfast Inn is one of those off-the-beaten-track discoveries that we felt compelled to share. The smallest of our recommended Sedona-area hideaways, The Graham Inn is situated in a residential area and might easily be mistaken for another private home.

Holding only a half-dozen rooms, the inn pampers guests with amenities like videocassette players, custom tile, and spa tubs for two in a contemporary Southwest atmosphere. Views of towering sandstone pinnacles with names like Satan's Arch and Wildhorse Mesa are offered from some guest rooms as well as from the backyard swimming pool and spa.

ROOMS FOR ROMANCE
We enjoyed a night in the Sedona Suite (around $200), the inn's most expensive room and one of the region's most stunning romantic accommodations. A favorite among honeymooners, the suite boasts a fabulous room-sized bath with Mexican *saltillo* tile, two vanities, a spa tub for two, and a large separate shower with dual heads.

The carpeted bedroom holds a king-sized Taos bed and a television with a videocassette player. (The inn maintains a sizable movie collection.) The tiled living room has a woodburning fireplace and cushioned wicker chairs; a private outdoor patio, which faces Satan's Arch, is furnished with a table and chairs.

The art deco–style San Francisco Room (upper $100 range) features an artfully designed, platform king-sized bed, a gas fireplace, a chaise longue, and a sunset-view balcony. A huge marble spa tub for two also awaits here. A videocassette player and television are tucked behind a picture above the fireplace.

Another romantic favorite is the Southwest Room (mid $100 range), a cozy retreat furnished with a queen-sized Taos bed, a love seat, a woodburning fireplace with hand-painted tiles, and interesting objets d'art. There's a spa tub for two in the bathroom and a balcony with a scenic red rock view.

The Champagne Suite (mid $100 range) has a gas fireplace and an oversized shower with dual heads. The least expensive room, Garden, has an oversized oval-shaped soaking tub and is offered in the low $100 range.

Casa Sedona

55 Hozoni Drive

Sedona, AZ 86336

Telephone: (520) 282-2938; toll-free: (800) 525-3756

Fifteen rooms, each with private bath, fireplace, and spa tub for one or two. Complimentary full breakfast served at tables for two in the dining room, at outdoor terrace tables, or in your room. Handicapped access. Smoking is not permitted anywhere on property. Two-night minimum stay required during weekends. Moderate to expensive.

Getting There

From Interstate 17 (two hours from Phoenix), exit at Highway 179 and drive north fifteen miles to Sedona. In downtown Sedona, turn left on Highway 89A and follow three miles to Southwest Drive. Turn right on Southwest Drive and follow as it curves left. Turn right on Hozoni Drive and follow to inn's driveway at end of road.

Casa Sedona ⋄ *Sedona*

I t's one of the town's newest inns, but Casa Sedona has quickly emerged as one of the most popular, especially among romancing couples. From a creature comfort perspective, Casa Sedona is, in our opinion, the community's most romantic hideaway. The only feature lacking is a swimming pool.

Designed by a protégé of Frank Lloyd Wright, the Southwestern-style inn is set discreetly at the end of a road on a very scenic spot, offering guests enchanting views of the native landscape and the mountains. Mongollon Rim, visible from many of the rooms, changes color throughout the day as the sun rises and falls.

The inn's rural setting offers visiting couples the option of setting off on day hikes directly from the Casa Sedona property. If trekking isn't on your itinerary, sit under a backyard shade tree and soak up the atmosphere. And Sedona shops are just a quick drive away.

Rooms for Romance

With red rock views, fireplaces, and spa tubs for two offered with every room, it's difficult to pick favorites here. However, the luscious Sunset Suite (upper $100 range) is one of the inn's most popular accommodations. Facing the rear of the property, the suite holds a cozy couch and a separate shower as well as the aforementioned romantic amenities.

Esmerelda (mid $100 range) is a corner room from which majestic Thunder Mountain is visible. The room has a corner fireplace and a terrace that affords pretty sunset vistas.

Anasazi and Kachina (upper $100 range) have private sunset-view terraces, and Hozoni (mid $100 range) has a private deck.

Safari (upper $100 range) features a handsome African motif, and Sunset (upper $100 range) has a pretty sleigh bed and offers romantic evening views.

L'Auberge de Sedona

301 L'Auberge Lane

Sedona, AZ 86336

Telephone: (520) 282-1661

Fifty-seven rooms, each with private bath. Swimming
pool and restaurant. Handicapped access. Smoking
is not permitted. Two-night minimum stay required
during weekends and holiday periods. Deluxe.

Getting There

From Interstate 17 (two hours from Phoenix), exit at
Highway 179 and drive north fifteen miles to Sedona.
At the intersection of Highways 179 and 89A, turn
right onto Highway 89A. Immediately on the right is
the Cedars Resort, and next to it is a small street sign
for L'Auberge Lane. Follow the lane to the right and
into the resort.

Visitors to L'Auberge de Sedona who are unaccustomed to living in the lap of sinful luxury will likely feel the same guilty pleasure that comes with sliding behind the wheel of an expensive sports car or diving into a bowl of Häagen-Dazs ice cream. Lolling in our sumptuous room, floating in the pool while gazing at the distant red rugged landscape, and dining by the serene creek, we wondered whether anyone was really worthy of such an experience.

Set along Oak Creek amid trees and gardens, the resort engenders a feeling of delightful seclusion, although the bustling Tlaquepaque Arts and Crafts Village is only a short walk away. We'd guess that most Sedona visitors aren't even aware of this delicious canyon resort hidden just off the main road.

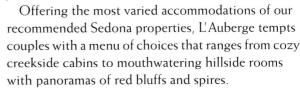

Offering the most varied accommodations of our recommended Sedona properties, L'Auberge tempts couples with a menu of choices that ranges from cozy creekside cabins to mouthwatering hillside rooms with panoramas of red bluffs and spires.

While making a decision may prove daunting, you can at least take comfort in knowing that it's impossible to go wrong, no matter where you ultimately unpack your bags. And you can always come again to sample another L'Auberge hideaway.

Rooms for Romance

We'll start with the cottages, an enchanting collection of more than two dozen French country gems that are clustered along or near the rushing creek. These all have deep carpeting, wrought-iron canopy beds, cushy love seats, fireplaces, and porches.

We spent a warm summer night in Cottage 2, set on a grassy knoll under a canopy of trees and overlooking melodious Oak Creek. Our covered front porch held two cushioned pine log chairs and a cozy love seat. Inside was a spacious, carpeted living room with a fireplace, a couch, a table and chairs, and a cassette/compact disc player. The two bedrooms each held a queen-sized iron bed.

Cottages 5 and 6 are the most remote of the creek-facing units. Cottages 1 through 4 all face the creek and lawn. At the upper part of the property, Cottages 15 through 19 occupy a sandy creekside spot. One-bedroom cottages are offered in the high $200 range; two-bedroom cottages fetch approximately $400. Rates are considerably lower from mid-November through February.

Another option is the European-style lodge, situated near the center of the property. This attractive building houses a dramatic lobby and conference rooms, as well as several guest rooms (mid to upper $100 range) with king-sized canopy beds.

If you're more interested in red rock romance, we suggest a room in the Orchards building, which sits atop the hillside above the cottages and lodge. Connected to the canyon floor by a funicular, the Orchards consists of nicely appointed rooms (mid to upper $100 range), some with fireplaces, and each with a balcony or patio offering dramatic mountain vistas. Set at street level, the Orchards provides direct and quick access to Sedona shops.

THE LODGE AT SEDONA

125 Kallof Place

Sedona, AZ 86336

Telephone: (520) 204-1942; toll-free: (800) 619-4467

Thirteen rooms, each with private bath. Complimentary full breakfast served at tables for two and four or in your room. Weekend dinner service available. Handicapped access. Smoking is not permitted. Two-night minimum stay required during weekends and holiday periods. Moderate to deluxe.

Getting There

From Interstate 17 (two hours from Phoenix), exit at Highway 179 and drive north fifteen miles to Sedona. In downtown Sedona, turn left on Highway 89A and follow for two miles. Turn left on Kallof Place and follow to inn.

The Lodge at Sedona is a labor of love for innkeepers Barb and Mark Dinunzio, who created this cozy romantic hideaway as newlyweds. Shortly after it opened in 1993, it was named by *The Arizona Republic* as the state's best bed-and-breakfast inn.

Described by an early visitor as "drop-dead delish," the Lodge underwent considerable cosmetic surgery before welcoming couples for romantic getaways. Built in 1959 for a family of fourteen, the home later served as a residence for elderly ladies and was eventually purchased by a local hospital, which turned it into an inpatient treatment center. To bring their vision to life, the Dinunzios worked for months, installing 250 sheets of dry wall to help ensure privacy and adding eight and a half bathrooms so that no guest would have to trudge "down the hall."

Tucked away in a nice neighborhood and almost hidden behind fragrant pine trees, the two-story property still resembles a comfortable family home. Inside, guests will discover a variety of inviting public spaces and a very friendly tone set by Barb and Mark.

ROOMS FOR ROMANCE

There's a tie between the Master Suite and the Tea Rose Suite for the "most romantic room" award. The Master Suite, at around $200, is the inn's most expensive room. Brick arches and a red rock fireplace lend a somewhat masculine accent to this spacious and attractive downstairs suite, which has a private entrance. Furnishings include a queen-sized pine bed, a matching armoire, and a wicker love seat. The bathroom has double sinks and a spa tub-and-shower combination, and a private deck holds your own tub for two.

The Tea Rose Suite, which is priced a few dollars less, has an elegant bathroom with spa tub for two. An archway separates the bedroom from the sitting room, which is furnished with a love seat and a gas fireplace. French doors open to a patio.

Another recommended room is Renaissance (mid $100 range), an upstairs room under the eaves with a queen-sized brass-and-iron bed and a dormer window seat. In the vintage-style bathroom is a small clawfoot tub with a shower extension and a pedestal sink.

Paisley (low to mid $100 range), a downstairs room, has a king-sized bed, spa tub, rich dark woods, and a view deck. The cowboy-themed Lariat Room (around $100) is filled with whimsical Western memorabilia, including a cardboard cutout of John Wayne. Saloon doors open to the bathroom, equipped with a shower. The sink is placed in the room. This second-floor room has a red-rock view.

ENCHANTMENT RESORT
525 Boynton Canyon Road
Sedona, AZ 86336
Telephone: (520) 282-2900; toll-free: (800) 826-4180

One hundred sixty-two rooms and suites, each with
private bath. Complimentary orange juice and newspaper delivered to your room each morning. Swimming pools, tennis courts, golf course, croquet course,
spa, restaurant, and lounge. Handicapped access.
Smoking is allowed. Two-night minimum stay
required during weekends; three-night minimum
during holiday periods. Deluxe.

Getting There
From Interstate 17 (two hours from Phoenix), exit at
Highway 179 and drive north fifteen miles to Sedona.
In downtown Sedona, turn left on Highway 89A and
follow for three miles. Turn right on Dry Creek Road
and follow to Boynton Canyon Road. Turn right and
follow to resort. Office is on the left.

ENCHANTMENT RESORT ❖ *Sedona*

Those who require proof that a magical energy pervades the Sedona area need only experience Enchantment Resort to become, well, enchanted. From our private, east-facing patio, the two of us sat silent and awestruck as a setting winter sun painted looming canyon walls with a changing palette of hypnotic hues. Strolling onto the darkened patio after dinner, we were greeted with another masterpiece: the dazzling night sky.

During our Sedona sojourns, we've not discovered a retreat that better showcases the region's mountain majesty than Enchantment Resort. If you're only able to stay, heaven forbid, one night in Sedona, we recommend you spend it here.

The resort has a Sedona address, but it's actually situated about five scenic miles from town, hidden in rugged Boynton Canyon and presided over by trees and towering sandstone walls. It's a full-service destination, offering a dozen tennis courts, four swimming pools, outdoor spas, a six-hole golf course, a croquet court, a spa and fitness center, and a restaurant. There's also an outdoor deck on the roof of the clubhouse for panoramic views of the twinkling heavens. Hiking trails along the canyon walls lead to ancient ruins and caves.

ROOMS FOR ROMANCE

Dotting the seventy-acre property are dozens of Southwestern-style *casitas*, most housing three units each. Guests may choose from two-bedroom suites (upper $300 range), one-bedroom suites (upper $200 range), deluxe studio suites (mid $200 range), and "guest bedrooms" (around $200). All rooms—there are more than 150 in all—have private patios, telephones, televisions, and coffeemakers.

The one- and two-bedroom and deluxe studio suites all have patio barbeques, fireplaces, couches, and kitchenettes. Guest bedrooms do not.

The spacious deluxe studio suites contain queen-sized Murphy beds, living areas, and dining areas, in addition to the aforementioned features.

Guest bedrooms hold either king- or queen-sized beds and a couple of cushioned chairs. Our cozy guest bedroom (Room 340), which suited us just fine, held two queen-sized beds whose quilted headboards matched the spreads. The well-equipped bathroom had double sinks, and the elevated patio was very private, providing straight-on views of the canyon walls.

51

GARLAND'S OAK CREEK LODGE

P.O. Box 152

Sedona, AZ 86336

Telephone (answered from March through mid-
November): (520) 282-3343

Sixteen cabins, each with private bath. Modified
American plan rates include full breakfast and dinner,
as well as afternoon snacks. Tennis court and dining
room. Handicapped access. Smoking is allowed.
Two-night minimum stay required. Closed mid-
November through March. Moderate to expensive.

Getting There

From Sedona, drive north on Highway 89A for
eight miles and turn left at the lodge's sign at Banjo
Bill Campground, cross the creek (right through
the water), and drive a short distance to the lodge.
Garland's is twenty miles south of Flagstaff.

GARLAND'S
☉ OAK CREEK LODGE ❖ *Sedona*

J ust because Garland's is one of Oak Creek Canyon's best-kept secrets, don't assume you can call today for a reservation next weekend. Consider yourself lucky if you can book a night anytime this year, or next for that matter. Former guests have first right of refusal for the same time next year, and there's typically a waiting list of hungry travelers poised for cancellations, which do occur frequently. Although the lodge is open from April through mid-November, they do not begin taking phone reservations till March; from mid-November to February, you'll need to write.

A small, family-run resort consisting of sixteen simple but charming cabins, Garland's is set deep in a wooded gorge about eight miles north of Sedona. You reach this idyllic spot by crossing Oak Creek by foot, not car. The creek's famous slide rocks are nearby.

The lodge's dining room serves highly rated "nouvelle American" dinners of a half dozen or so courses, which are just about as popular as the cozy cabins. The management promises to "awaken you in time for dinner," but don't miss the glorious breakfasts where Oak Creek trout, corn oysters, or banana pancakes might be included on the day's menu. Rates noted below include a full breakfast and dinner for two.

ROOMS FOR ROMANCE

Because vacancies are rare, you're not likely to have the opportunity to choose your own cabin, but traveling romantics needn't worry. All accommodations are suitable for snuggling.

We happened by during a quiet springtime week just before the resort opened for the season, and we were able to peek inside several of the knotty-pine-paneled cabins. Bathrooms are modern and appropriately equipped with showers, and all of the cabins have porches with comfortable chairs. There are no telephones, radios, or televisions to distract you from the scenery.

Cabins are classified as either large (upper $100 range) or small (mid $100 range). The large cabins have a bed sitting room, a fireplace, and either one king-sized bed or two extra-long double beds. Some of the smaller romantic cabins sit along a bluff overlooking the creek. Others are situated in a more remote orchard on a hill above the main compound.

The Inn at 410

410 North Leroux Street
Flagstaff, AZ 86001
Telephone: (520) 774-0088; toll-free: (800) 774-2008

Eight rooms, each with private bath; two with spa
tubs for two; three with fireplaces. Complimentary
full breakfast served in dining room or continental
breakfast delivered to your room. Handicapped access.
Smoking is not permitted. Two-night minimum stay
required during weekends from April through October.
Moderate.

Getting There
Interstate 17 north becomes Milton Road in Flagstaff.
In downtown Flagstaff, follow northbound Milton as
it curves right and becomes Santa Fe Avenue (Route
66). Turn left on Leroux Street and follow four blocks
up the hill to inn on right.

THE INN AT 410 ❖ *Flagstaff*

In the early 1970s, visitors to 410 North Leroux Street were more likely looking for a beer bust or a toga party than a quiet romantic overnight interlude. These days, the atmosphere at this former fraternity house is considerably more sedate, the rousing choruses of "Louie Louie" having been replaced by the crackling of a fire and hushed conversations among traveling couples. Visitors aren't even disturbed by televisions or telephones.

Just a few years shy of its centennial, this tidy, well-preserved, two-story brick home served as a family residence for several generations. After its stint as a Northern Arizona University frat

house, the property was converted into apartments. It became an inn in the early 1990s.

Innkeepers Howard and Sally Krueger, who traded Chicago for Flagstaff in 1993, have made some romantic improvements that include enlarged rooms, in-room tubs for two, and fireplaces.

Situated in a clean and quiet neighborhood only a couple of blocks above Flagstaff's downtown shops and restaurants, the gray-and-white inn has sunny and inviting public areas and a canvas-covered patio for outdoor relaxing. A full breakfast is served at a communal table and tables for two, or a continental breakfast can be delivered to your room.

ROOMS FOR ROMANCE

Both offered in the low to mid $100 range, the Southwest Room and Tea Room are without question the inn's most romantic accommodations. The Southwest is a grand first-floor suite with brick walls, French doors, a white plaster fireplace, a couch, and a queen-sized Taos-style bed. The bathroom has a spa tub for two.

The home's original mahogany paneling is one of two intriguing features of the Tea Room. The other is a collection of teapots. This room has a king-sized bed and a fireplace, and the bathroom has a spa tub for two. Sunflower Fields (low $100 range), a queen-bedded room, is also equipped with a fireplace.

The Dakota (around $100) is a two-bedroom suite furnished in a Western theme, and it features a love seat and a queen-sized bed with a twig headboard. The other bedroom has two twin beds.

For bargain hunters, Room With a View was being offered at less than $100 at the time of our visit. Furnished with a queen-sized bed and offering a private bathroom, this room is on the second floor and faces Flagstaff. The sunset views are a bonus.

EL TOVAR HOTEL

South Rim

c/o Grand Canyon National Park Lodges

P.O. Box 699

Grand Canyon, AZ 86023

Telephone: (520) 638-2401

Sixty-five rooms, each with private bath. Restaurant and lounge. Dinner reservations advised. Handicapped access. Smoking is allowed; nonsmoking rooms available. No minimum stay requirement. Moderate to deluxe.

Getting There

From Phoenix, follow Interstate 17 north to Flagstaff. In Flagstaff, drive west on Interstate 40 to Williams. From Williams, drive north on Highways 64/180 to Grand Canyon Village; hotel is on right.

EL TOVAR HOTEL ❖ *The Grand Canyon*

Considered the jewel of the Grand Canyon, El Tovar Hotel has been treating visitors to memorable canyon vistas and vacations since just after the turn of the century.

Inspired by European hunting lodges, the rustic yet stately hostelry was named in memory of Don Pedro de Tovar, a Spanish explorer who happened upon this beautiful spot long ago.

The hotel's interior and exterior architecture is stunning. Native stone, massive beams, and log walls are used extensively throughout the public areas. Fireplaces abound. One of the favorite gathering spots is El Tovar Lounge, where a pianist entertains after dark.

ROOMS FOR ROMANCE

El Tovar, which offers the canyon's most deluxe overnight experience, classifies its rooms as standard double-bed rooms (low $100 range); standard queen bed rooms (low to mid $100 range); deluxe (mid $100 range); and suites, which span from the high $100 range to the high $200 range.

We recommend either deluxe rooms or suites.

El Tovar advertises four suites (upper $200 range) as having dramatic canyon views. Other rooms may have a peek of the canyon, but since you can't request a specific room number, it's the luck of the draw.

Bright Angel Lodge and Cabins

South Rim
c/o Grand Canyon National Park Lodges
P.O. Box 699
Grand Canyon, AZ 86023
Telephone: (520) 638-2401

Seventy-one rooms and cabins, most with private baths.
Two restaurants, lounge, and gift shop. Handicapped
access. Smoking is allowed; non-smoking rooms available.
No minimum-stay requirement. Moderate.

Getting There
From Phoenix, follow Interstate 17 north to Flagstaff. In
Flagstaff, drive west on Interstate 40 to Williams. From
Williams, drive north on Highways 64/180 to Grand
Canyon Village; lodge is on right just past El Tovar.

BRIGHT ANGEL LODGE AND CABINS ÷ *The Grand Canyon*

Perched on the south rim in the shadow of the more famous El Tovar, Bright Angel Lodge is a less-expensive Grand Canyon lodging alternative and one that offers a more rustic experience.

The second oldest lodge on the south rim, Bright Angel includes not only standard guest rooms but a collection of popular, rim-hugging cabins that can be yours for a night or two at a relative bargain.

ROOMS FOR ROMANCE

Many of the little cabins (around $100) are situated dramatically close to the canyon's edge, while others have less inspiring locations. Some of the cabins even have fireplaces.

Traveling romantics need to keep in mind that some of the cabins are old, rustic, and fairly basic. It's only a step or two away from a camping experience, so don't expect the Ritz. Also, the popular canyon rim walkway skirts this property, and there usually are lots of camera- and ice cream cone–toting tourists around during the daytime.

Compared to our other featured destinations, the anonymous lodge building is architecturally lackluster, and the rooms can best be described as standard. However, some do have great views of the Grand Canyon. Lodge rooms are offered for less than $100.

Southern New Mexico

Daytime Diversions

The Space Center, located in Alamogordo, pays tribute to space exploration with displays and replicas.

At Cloudcroft, an all-season resort area, Snow Canyon (two miles from the Lodge) beckons with downhill and cross-country skiing and snowmobiling in winter. The warmer months bring mountain bikers and golfers to this high-altitude escape.

Every October, the streets of Las Cruces heat up with the popular Enchilada Festival, a wild, three-day-long fiesta during which the world's largest enchilada is created.

Two miles away from Las Cruces is Mesilla, a carefully preserved historic New Mexican town with galleries, restaurants, and shops.

Sierra Mesa Lodge is located close to the Ski Apache ski basin, the nation's southernmost ski area, and is also near Lincoln National Forest. Guests at the Lodge may also participate in murder mystery weekends.

The southern New Mexico region is also home to Carlsbad Caverns National Park and White Sands National Monument.

Tables for Two

Tatsu, 930 East Paseo Road, Las Cruces
Double Eagle, 308 Calle de Guadalupe, Mesilla
Rebecca's, The Lodge, Cloudcroft (see separate listing in this section)
Victoria's Romantic Hideaway, 2103 Sudderth, Ruidoso
La Lorraine, 2523 Sudderth, Ruidoso

Lundeen Inn of the Arts

618 South Alameda Boulevard
Las Cruces, NM 88005
Telephone: (505) 526-3327

Twenty rooms, each with private bath. Complimentary breakfast served at large communal table, tables for two, or in your room. Art gallery. Handicapped access. Smoking is allowed. Two-night minimum stay during holiday periods. Moderate.

Getting There
From southbound Interstate 25, take the Lohman exit and turn right. Follow for approximately five miles and turn left on Alameda Boulevard. Inn is on the right.

Lundeen Inn
☉ of the Arts ⁘ *Las Cruces*

Jerry and Linda Lundeen run what you might call a full-service inn for romantics. Not only does the couple set the stage for a romantic weekend with their romantic decor, Jerry can write a personal marriage ceremony and pronounce you husband and wife on the spot.

A North Dakota native reared on an Indian reservation, Jerry is a lay minister (as well as an architect) who frequently ties the knot for romantic travelers. Linda, also born and raised in New Mexico, operates the inn's art gallery.

The Lundeens' establishment is itself a marriage of sorts. Two-hundred-year-old adobes were creatively joined by Jerry to create Inn of the Arts, and the patio that separated them became the inn's soaring living room. This room, called the Merienda, also functions occasionally as a classroom when area artists, craftspeople, actors, and writers conduct seminars and lectures.

Rooms for Romance

The Ken Barrick and Tony Hillerman rooms (low $100 range) are two adjacent, freestanding, century-old *casitas* that are favorites among couples seeking romantic and private retreats. Barrick has a full kitchen, a fireplace, a queen-sized bed, and a private courtyard patio. The Hillerman Room holds a fireplace that was designed by Jerry in addition to a full kitchen.

In the main building, the Olaf Weighorst Room (low $100 range) features two queen-sized beds and a woodburning stove. In the bathroom, a red clawfoot tub with a shower extension is draped in netting.

The guest room pictured here is the Maria Martinez Room (under $100), one of the Southwest's romantic bargains. This sunny room has a fireplace and dark hardwood floors, and it's lit from south- and west-facing windows. It overlooks the garden and the adobe gazebo. The bathroom has *saltillo* tiles and a tub-and-shower combination.

Georgia O'Keeffe (under $100) is a popular second-floor room with a balcony and an unusual, antique freestanding mantel into which the bed has been placed.

Artist R. C. Gorman's namesake room has a private entrance, a kiva fireplace, and a partial viga ceiling, as well as a cozy built-in seating nook.

THE LODGE AT CLOUDCROFT
1 Corona Place
Cloudcroft, NM 88317
Telephone toll-free: (800) 395-6343

Sixty rooms, each with private bath. Restaurant, swimming pool, spa, sauna, and nine-hole links-style golf course. No handicapped access. Smoking is allowed in designated areas. No minimum stay requirement. Moderate to deluxe.

Getting There
From Alamogordo on Highway 54, follow Highway 82 east for approximately sixteen miles. Watch for signs to the Lodge.

THE LODGE
AT CLOUDCROFT ❖ *Cloudcroft*

In each region we've visited in search of romantic getaways, we have discovered at least one lodging with a nonpaying spiritual guest. At the Lodge, we heard about but did not meet Rebecca, a ghostly guest who in real life was an unfortunate victim of romance.

As the story goes, Rebecca was a pretty, red-haired Lodge chambermaid who vanished in the 1930s after a jealous boyfriend discovered her with another. These days, Rebecca's ghost is occasionally seen in the hallways and in Room 101, purportedly in search of a new lover. Ladies, keep an eye on your partners! Rebecca's name also graces the inn's respected restaurant.

Boasting a guest list that's as eclectic as its fabled façade, the Lodge has played host over the years to such notables as Pancho Villa and Judy Garland. Rebuilt in 1911 after a fire, the restored structure features a beautiful setting and a nearly nine-thousand-foot elevation. A fourth-floor copper-domed observatory affords one-hundred-fifty-mile views across White Sands National Monument. The Lodge is surrounded by the Lincoln National Forest.

ROOMS FOR ROMANCE
The handful of west-facing front rooms have the best views, but the inn won't make specific reservations based on the view.

You may, however, put in a special request for the Honeymoon Suite (high $100 range), done in romantic reds and golds. This luscious retreat has a king-sized bed with four curved posts and an ornate gold crown. The bathroom, open to the room, has a spa tub for two surrounded by mirrors.

Every New Mexican governor has sampled the Governor's Suite (high $100 range), appointed with antiques and a queen-sized four-poster bed.

About half a mile away is a separate Lodge-run building called the Pavillion, which holds ten more rustic and oft-requested rooms with private entries. One of these, Room 505B (around $100), has a king-sized bed and a fireplace.

Sierra Mesa Lodge

Fort Stanton Road
Alto, NM 88312
Telephone: (505) 336-4515

Five rooms, each with private bath. Complimentary full breakfast served at communal table or in your room. Indoor spa. No handicapped access. Smoking is not permitted. Two- to three-night minimum stay required during holiday periods. Moderate.

Getting There
From Interstate 25 at San Antonio, drive east on Highway 380 and follow through Carrizozo. Turn south on Highway 37 and follow past Nogal to Highway 48. Drive south on Highway 48 to Alto Village. Turn left on Sierra Blanca Regional Airport Road (Highway D220) and follow for two miles to Fort Stanton Road. Turn right and follow to inn on right. The inn is six miles north of downtown Ruidoso.

SIERRA MESA LODGE ✢ *Alto*

Don't be fooled by the homelike façade of this lovely blue-and-white mountain retreat. It's not one of those home-turned-inn conversions that is short on privacy and long on inconvenience. It took former art director Larry Goodman and his accountant wife, Lila, more than a dozen years to find just the right spot and design their very romantic New Mexican bed-and-breakfast inn.

Open since 1987, Sierra Mesa Lodge is only about a ten-minute drive from Ruidoso, set against a hillside under tall trees. The inn enjoys a cool seven-thousand-foot elevation and borders on the Lincoln National Forest.

Although guest rooms do not contain televisions or telephones, the TV addicted do have access to an upstairs TV room, which also contains a telescope.

In the public spa room, which has a view, guests clad in kimonos provided in their rooms need only hang the privacy sign to enjoy a secluded soak.

ROOMS FOR ROMANCE

At the time of our travels, rates for each of the five themed rooms were right around $100, including afternoon dessert and a full breakfast that can be taken in the dining room or enjoyed in your room. Each room has a window seat, a comforter, and goose down pillows. To ensure privacy, interior walls have been generously insulated. The little porcelain China dolls that grace each guest room were all handmade by Lila, whose two passions are cooking and dollmaking.

A lacy queen-sized four-poster bed and a chaise longue are among the romantic appointments of the English-styled Queen Anne Room, and French Country has a handsome French Quarter–style bed and a small sitting area.

The Victorian Room holds a pretty, queen-sized, white-iron and brass bed, antique oak furniture, and a stylish Victorian fainting couch. The bathroom has a clawfoot tub-and-shower combination.

A completely different environment awaits in the Oriental Room, carpeted in gray and featuring a queen-sized bed with a dark canopied bonnet and a mirrored headboard. At one end of the room hangs a colorful marriage robe.

A high, queen-sized, pineapple-post step-up bed is the centerpiece of the Country Western Room, which is also furnished with a rocking chair and country decor.

NORTHERN NEW MEXICO

Daytime Diversions

The famous Santa Fe Opera, held in an open-air auditorium seven miles north of Santa Fe, typically runs from July through late August. For summer daytime excitement, ask your Santa Fe innkeeper about Rio Grande or Rio Chama rafting trips. During the winter months, locals and visitors head for the Santa Fe Ski Area in the Sangre de Cristo Mountains about sixteen miles northeast of Santa Fe.

The Taos area, famous for skiing as well as art, is the home of Taos Ski Valley, with some of the nation's most challenging skiing. The Taos Pueblo, just two miles from town, is the largest existing multistoried pueblo structure in the United States. Residents conduct informal tours for daytime visitors. Taos Plaza, in the heart of town, is surrounded by interesting shops and eateries. The Kit Carson Home and Museum and the Millicent Rogers Museum are each worth a visit. And you won't travel more than a few steps in Taos without stumbling on an art gallery. At last count there were around eighty.

In Albuquerque, we recommend a stroll through Old Town and the thrilling two-and-a-half-mile ride on the nation's longest aerial tram along Sandia Peak.

Those romantic New Mexican Christmas celebrations, when flickering *farolitos* and *luminarias* light the crisp night sky, generally run from early December into January.

Tables for Two

Cafe de las Placitas, 664 Highway 165, Placitas
  (a half hour north of Albuquerque)
Monte Vista Fire Station, 3201 Central
  Avenue NE, Albuquerque
Coyote Cafe, 132 West Water Street, Santa Fe
La Casa Sena Restaurant, 125 East Palace Avenue,
  Santa Fe
Santacafe, 231 Washington Avenue, Santa Fe
The Apple Tree, 123 Bent Street, Taos
Villa Fontana, 71 Highway 522, five miles
  north of Taos

Casas de Sueños

310 Rio Grande Boulevard SW
Albuquerque, NM 87104
Telephone: (505) 247-4560; toll-free: (800) 242-8987

Seventeen rooms, each with private bath; five with
fireplaces. Complimentary full breakfast served at
tables for two. Handicapped access. Smoking is not
permitted. Two-night minimum stay required during
weekends; three-night minimum during holiday
periods. Moderate to deluxe.

Getting There
From Interstate 40 in Albuquerque, exit at Rio Grande
Boulevard and drive south past the third stoplight for
two blocks to inn on left.

CASAS DE SUEÑOS ❖ *Albuquerque*

The folks at Casas de Sueños recall with pride the story of a couple who, after exchanging wedding vows on the inn's enchanting grounds, bid their families and friends goodbye and departed under the traditional shower of rice. Purportedly bound for some distant honeymoon destination, the cunning couple instead drove around the block and, unbeknownst to the wedding guests, quietly snuggled into La Miradora, the inn's honeymoon suite.

After touring the cozy rooms and the lush gardens of Casas de Sueños, we understood why the inn has become not only a favorite wedding site but a choice honeymoon destination. In our opinion, this is Albuquerque's most romantic inn. And it doesn't hurt that famous Old Town is only three blocks away.

Once an artists' compound, Casas de Sueños is by no means a predictable or typical bed-and-breakfast inn. The guest rooms, which used to be private residences, are delight-fully diverse, and some of the architecture—the snail-shaped building that greets arriving guests, for example—is a bit quirky. Spring and summer visitors will find the interior courtyard and gardens in colorful bloom.

ROOMS FOR ROMANCE

You walk under a grape arbor to enter Elliot Porter's Cottage (mid $100 range), one of our favorites. Located at the center of the gardens, this freestanding accommodation has a drawing room with a love seat, a kitchen, and a small bathroom with an unusual marble soaking tub. French doors lead from the bedroom to a private courtyard with a hot tub.

A separate room with a soft-sided six-foot spa is the main attraction of the Sueños Room (high $100 range), which faces a grassy courtyard. The room has a king-sized bed, and the bathroom is equipped with a tub-and-shower combination.

A garden waterfall in your private courtyard sends romantically soothing sounds through La Cascada (low $100 range), a two-room unit with a queen-sized, four-poster rattan bed and a separate sitting room.

La Miradora (low to mid $200 range), definitely for special occasions, is a large residence with two bedrooms and a drawing room that overlooks the adjacent Albuquerque Country Club. The suite has *viga* ceilings, a corner kiva fireplace, antiques, and an outdoor porch swing. The small tiled bathroom holds a large spa tub for two.

The Taos and Zuni rooms are located in a carriage house that, in our opinion, occupies a less desirable spot outside the main compound.

The Galisteo Inn

9 La Vega Road
Galisteo, NM 87540
Telephone: (505) 466-4000

Twelve rooms, eight with private baths; four with woodburning fireplaces. Complimentary buffet breakfast served in dining room. Swimming pool, hot tub, sauna, horseback riding, and fixed-price dinners. Handicapped access. Smoking is not permitted inside the inn. Two-night minimum stay required during high-season weekends; three-night minimum during holiday periods. Closed first five to six weeks of the year. Moderate to expensive.

Getting There

From Santa Fe, follow Interstate 25 north and exit at Highway 285. Drive south to Lamy and turn south on Highway 41. Follow to Galisteo. At the old Nuestra Señora de los Remidos Church, turn left and follow Via la Puente for a tenth of a mile. Turn left on La Vega Road and follow two-tenths of a mile to inn's driveway on right. Galisteo is twenty-three miles from Santa Fe.

The distance between the crumbling old adobes of Galisteo village and the sumptuous Galisteo Inn is less than one mile, but we felt as though we had traveled back a few hundred years in a time machine.

Actually, the contrast turned out to be somewhat less significant than our first impression indicated. The inn, we were told, was created from a hacienda that was built in the mid 1700s, making the Galisteo Inn the oldest of our fifty featured destinations.

Although there are some reminders of days gone by, like the old jail that stands on the property, don't expect a drafty old room and earthen floors. The years, not to mention the innkeepers, have been kind to the historic structure, which has been completely refurbished and updated over time.

The inn is accessed via a tree-shaded gravel road that runs from the authentic old hamlet of Galisteo past comfortable Southwestern-style family homes. Pasture and lawn surround the rambling, single-story inn, which is shaded by towering cottonwood trees.

Guests have access to a beautiful swimming pool and hot tub, but a sixty-three-hundred-foot elevation ensures a comfortable summer environment. There's also an indoor sauna.

There are no restaurants in the area, so most guests take advantage of the inn's fixed-price dinners, which are offered for around $60 per couple. Mountain bikes are available to guests at no extra charge.

ROOMS FOR ROMANCE

The most expensive room is Cottonwood (mid to upper $100 range), a separate and spacious cottage with a king-sized bed and a fireplace; it sits at the rear of the property facing a walled courtyard and the swimming pool. The tiled bathroom has double sinks.

Spruce (mid $100 range), the hacienda's original master bedroom, is also equipped with a king-sized bed and a fireplace. This corner room, which overlooks the front pasture with its sheep and horses, has a romantic double-headed shower.

Piñon (low to mid $100 range), reached from the inn's beautiful main hallway with *viga* ceilings and hardwood floors, has a fireplace and a queen-sized bed. Piñon also faces the pasture.

Located in a separate cottage, Birch (mid $100 range) is a sunny and bright room with picture windows that overlook the pasture. The room is equipped with a king-sized bed and a private patio.

The twin-bedded Cedar, Sycamore, and Oak rooms, and the double-bedded Juniper Room do not have private baths.

The Bishop's Lodge

Bishop's Lodge Road
Santa Fe, NM 87501
Telephone: (505) 983-6377

Eighty-eight rooms and suites, each with private bath;
forty-five with fireplaces. Swimming pool, spa, saunas,
exercise room, tennis courts, horseback riding, and
restaurant. Handicapped access. Smoking is allowed.
No minimum-stay requirement. Deluxe.

Getting There
From Albuquerque, drive north on Interstate 25, and
exit at St. Francis Drive/Highway 285. Drive seven
miles north and turn right on Camino Encantado.
Drive one mile, and turn left on Bishop's Lodge Road.
Drive one and a half miles to resort on right. From
the downtown plaza in Santa Fe, drive north on
Washington Avenue, which becomes Bishop's Lodge
Road. Follow three and a half miles to resort on right.

The Bishop's Lodge ❖ *Santa Fe*

Santa Fe visitors who'd like to put a little distance between themselves and the busy downtown area at the end of the day need only venture three miles up Bishop's Lodge Road, where this venerable resort has been offering respite since the 1920s.

The thousand-acre resort consists of eleven separate adobe-style "lodges" that dot gentle hillsides covered with native juniper and piñon as well as fruit trees. One of the most enchanting spots on the property is a romantic little adobe chapel reached by a footpath. Weddings are frequently held here.

Guests have access to a heated pool, a large indoor spa, an exercise room, and men's and women's saunas. There's an extra charge for tennis, skeet shooting, and horseback riding. The resort offers a free daily shuttle service to and from downtown Santa Fe.

Rates here are at their peak from July through Labor Day, when the resort bustles with families enjoying summer vacations above the desert heat. Tariffs are considerably less in the fall, winter, and spring, when you're more apt to see couples strolling the quiet grounds. For example, the deluxe rooms that receive our highest recommendation command over $300 during the summer. The same rooms are offered in the low $200 range at certain other times of the year. The resort is open year round.

Rooms for Romance

Although the resort's rooms are all comfortable, some of the older units we toured were fairly plain; a few were a bit dated. We were most consistently impressed with the Chamisa Lodge, and we recommend the rooms here for romantic getaways.

This two-story, pueblo-style building, built in 1994, holds more than a dozen spacious and contemporary-style rooms and occupies an attractive remote setting among the trees.

Among the accommodations here is Room 204, which overlooks an adjacent creek and trees. The wool-carpeted room is appointed with a couch, a craftsman-style chair, a corner gas kiva fireplace, and a king-sized bed, placed at an angle in a corner. The large tiled bath holds two sinks, a shower stall, and a deep soaking tub that just might hold both of you.

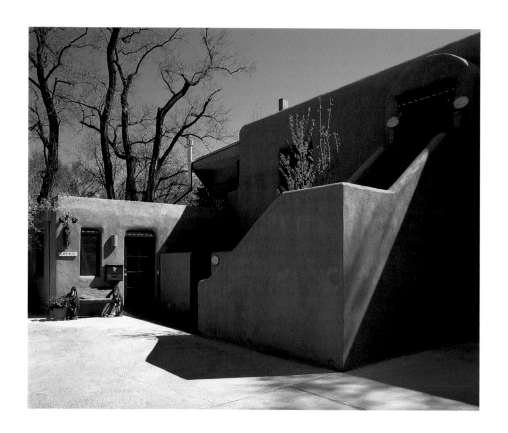

Dancing Ground of the Sun

711 Paseo de Peralta
Santa Fe, NM 87501
Telephone: (505) 986-9797; toll-free: (800) 645-5673

Five suites, each with private bath, kitchen, dining
room, telephone, and television; four have fireplaces.
Complimentary continental breakfast placed in refrigerator in your room. No handicapped access. Smoking
is not permitted. No minimum stay requirement.
Moderate to expensive.

Getting There
From Albuquerque, drive north on Interstate 25, and
exit at St. Francis Drive/Highway 285. Turn right on
Cerillos Road, then turn right on Paseo de Peralta and
follow as it curves to the left through Santa Fe. Inn is
on the right between Palace Avenue and Marcy
Street.

Dancing Ground
of the Sun ❖ *Santa Fe*

I t's not the appealing Taos-style furnishings, the corner kiva fireplaces, or the handsome viga ceilings that distinguish Dancing Ground of the Sun from Santa Fe's other romantic inns. It's that little balcony reached by climbing through a window, the washer and dryer in two rooms, the casual add-on here and there, and other endearing details that make this enclave of 1930s-era

pueblo-style bungalows stand out from the others. It's as close as an overnight visitor will get to actually living in casual and laid-back Santa Fe.

The five-unit inn, our Santa Fe favorite, occupies a shady spot at the edge of the downtown district, just three blocks from the plaza. Guests enter the property via a paved interior court that provides access to the rooms.

Rooms for Romance

The inn reflects the creative mastery of interior designer and innkeeper Connie Wristen, who has given each accommodation its own colorful and comfortable personality. Each suite is named after a native American spirit dancer, whose visage is carried from outdoor light fixtures to wastebaskets and tissue dispensers. All units have kitchens, compact disc and cassette players, and Taos-style sofas. Rates are in the mid $100 range.

Kokopelli, which is the inn's honeymoon suite, is a spacious one-bedroom casita with a dining room and a living room. The bedroom of this upstairs unit contains the inn's only king-sized bed and features the small balcony that's accessed by a window. Kokopelli also has a tiled fireplace.

Corn Dancer, the inn's smallest suite, has a queen-sized bed made of Aspen wood, placed next to an electric kiva fireplace. This upstairs unit with hardwood floors also has a separate dining area.

Two suites, Buffalo Dancer and Rainbow Dancer, face the busy road out front, but storm windows block most of the traffic noise, and the sleeping rooms face the quiet interior courtyard. These units each have a tiled kitchen, a fireplace, a washer and dryer, and comfortable dining and living rooms.

Clown Dancer, a more recent addition to the inn, is accessed through French doors from a private outdoor patio. The suite, which features tiled floors, has a large living room, a dining room, fireplace, and a spacious modern kitchen with white oak cabinetry.

THE DON GASPAR COMPOUND

623 Don Gaspar Avenue
Santa Fe, NM 87501
Telephone: (505) 986-8664

Six suites, each with private bath. Complimentary
continental breakfast brought to your suite each
morning. Handicapped access. Smoking is not
permitted. Two-night minimum stay required.
Moderate to deluxe.

Getting There

From Interstate 25, exit at Old Pecos Trail and drive
north into Santa Fe. Turn left on Paseo de Peralta,
then left on Don Gaspar Avenue. The compound is
one and a half blocks on the left. To reach the office,
follow Don Gaspar Avenue to the corner, turn left on
Booth Street and left at the alley. Park behind the
adobe wall and walk through the gate to the office.

THE DON GASPAR COMPOUND ⁘ *Santa Fe*

During a visit to the impressive Blue Lake Ranch in southwestern Colorado (see separate listing), innkeepers David and Shirley Alford mentioned casually that they also owned the Don Gaspar Compound in New Mexico. Impressed by what the couple had created in Colorado, we decided to take a look at the Santa Fe property. You'll be glad we did.

Set within an adobe-walled garden courtyard, the compound is located in the Don Gaspar Historic District, just a short distance from the state capitol and a mile or so from the downtown plaza.

ROOMS FOR ROMANCE

The Courtyard Casita (mid $100 range), a private apartment-sized suite with Mexican *saltillo* tile floors, boasts glorious floor-to-ceiling French windows in the living room that offer views of the garden fountain. French doors open onto a private patio, and there's a gas fireplace and a kitchen as well. The living room furniture, perfect for siestas, is overscaled and overstuffed. The bedroom contains a king-sized bed, and the bathroom is equipped with a spa tub for two.

The Fountain Casita (mid $100 range) also has *saltillo* tile floors, a gas fireplace, and a queen-sized bed. The fountain view through the living room's French doors is a romantic plus.

A separate adobe building houses the Southwest, Aspen, and Colorado suites. Southwest (mid $100 range) has a large adobe fireplace and a dining table for two in the living room. The bedroom holds a king-sized bed.

In Colorado (around $100), French doors open onto a patio. This suite has a nice-sized bedroom with a queen-sized bed and a sitting area that overlooks the garden. The kitchenette occupies a hallway alcove.

Aspen (mid $100 range) is a one-bedroom suite with a king-sized bed, a separate living room, and nice garden views through aspen trees.

There's also a three-bedroom, two-bathroom home that's rented as one unit to families or to couples traveling together.

PUEBLO BONITO

138 West Manhattan Avenue
Santa Fe, NM 87501
Telephone: (505) 984-8001; toll-free: (800) 461-4599

Eighteen rooms, each with private bath and wood-
burning fireplace. Complimentary continental
breakfast served at tables for two or in your room.
Indoor hot tub. Restaurant. Handicapped access.
Smoking is allowed. No minimum stay requirement.
Moderate to expensive.

Getting There
From Interstate 25, exit at Old Pecos Trail and drive
north into Santa Fe. Turn left on Paseo de Peralta,
turn right on Galisteo Street and follow to inn on
right at corner of Manhattan and Galisteo.

PUEBLO BONITO ⋄ *Santa Fe*

Traveling couples looking for a romantic room in Santa Fe that won't bust their budget will applaud our discovery of this pleasant inn just around the corner from the New Mexico state capitol. At the time of our visit, cozy rooms with woodburning corner kivas, traditional *viga* ceilings, and private baths were available during the spring, summer, and fall high season for around $100 per night, a relative bargain in this popular destination city. During winter months, rates are even more reasonable.

Formerly a grand private estate dating from the early 1900s, Pueblo Bonito now consists of eighteen renovated guest rooms, all of which are equipped with fireplaces.

Eleven rooms and a single suite are contained within a two-story building, while six suites are strung together along the rear of the property. Brick paths wind through lush courtyards and gardens, and adobe archways open onto the city streets.

A continental breakfast buffet is served either in the communal dining room or outdoors on the patio.

ROOMS FOR ROMANCE

According to the folks at Pueblo Bonito, Room 8 (mid $100 range), known as Comanche, is "everybody's favorite." This tight and cozy hideaway, the only suite contained in the two-story building, has its own front porch as well as a queen-sized bed and maple floors.

The other six suites (mid $100 range) are excellent choices as well. Each has a queen-sized bed, a separate sitting room with a sofa bed, a kiva fireplace, and a kitchen. The San Ildefonso Suite has its own backyard.

Dos Casas Viejas

610 Agua Fria Street
Santa Fe, NM 87501
Telephone: (505) 983-1636

Six rooms and suites, each with private bath and
woodburning kiva fireplace. Complimentary
continental breakfast served in dining room at tables
for two or may be taken to your room. Swimming
pool. Handicapped access. Smoking is not permitted.
Two-night minimum stay required during weekends;
three-night minimum during holiday periods.
Expensive to deluxe.

Getting There

From Albuquerque, drive north on Interstate 25, and
exit at St. Francis Drive/Highway 285; it's approximately four miles into Santa Fe. Turn right at Agua
Fria Street. Follow for two blocks to inn on right.

DOS CASAS VIEJAS ✤ *Santa Fe*

Don't be misled by the English translation of Dos Casas Viejas. It means "two old houses," but this is one of Santa Fe's most luxurious inns. It's arguably the city's most romantic as well.

An artful blend of old and new—a mix of Anglo, Indian, and Mexican cultures—Dos Casas Viejas combines vintage features like antique *viga* ceilings and Mexican armoires with contemporary private bathrooms and even a lap pool.

When not enjoying their own private indoor and outdoor spaces, guests can usually be found lounging around the forty-foot pool or relaxing in the adjacent public sitting room, with its warming fireplace, *viga* ceilings, cozy couches and built-in bookshelves. A tiled dining room is set with tables for two.

We're obliged to point out that this highly recommended inn isn't situated in one of Santa Fe's best neighborhoods, but the gated, high adobe walls create a completely private and enchanting environment.

ROOMS FOR ROMANCE

Rooms 1 and 4 (mid $100 range) are considered standard accommodations. Rooms 3 and 5 (around $200) are minisuites; Room 2 (also around $200) is a two-room suite. Room 6 (mid $200 range) is a deluxe suite with two rooms, two fireplaces, and two patios. All are suitable for romantic getaways.

All rooms are accessed via heavy, wooden Mexican-style doors, which open onto private brick patios with outdoor furniture. The patios all feature colorful flowers; hanging chile clusters, called *ristras*, hang outside. You'll enter your room from the patio through French doors. There is a raised woodburning kiva fireplace in each room, as well as romantic amenities like fresh flowers and candles.

One of the two least expensive accommodations, Room 4 has a queen-sized bed, pine floors, and a sitting nook with a window seat.

In Room 5, one of the two generously sized minisuites, the living area is separated from the bedroom by a cushioned built-in couch, which faces the kiva fireplace and two wing chairs. A spacious bathroom holds an antique bench and a tiled tub-and-shower combination. The bed is king-sized.

GRANT CORNER INN
122 Grant Avenue
Santa Fe, NM 87501
Telephone: (505) 983-6678

Twelve rooms, ten with private baths. Complimentary full breakfast served at tables for two and four in the dining room, on the deck, or in your room. Restaurant. Handicapped access. Smoking is not permitted. Three-night minimum stay required during holiday periods. Moderate to expensive.

Getting There
From Albuquerque, drive north on Interstate 25, and exit at St. Francis Drive/Highway 285; it's approximately four miles into Santa Fe. Turn right on Alameda, left on Guadalupe, and right on Johnson. The inn is on the corner of Grant and Johnson avenues.

GRANT CORNER INN ❖ *Santa Fe*

Displaying a stunning gabled façade that turns the heads of passing motorists and slows the strolls of all but the most determined pedestrians, Grant Corner Inn is one of Santa Fe's most well-known inns, famous not only for its beds but for its breakfasts as well. An afterthought at so many inns, the morning meal is one of the main attractions here. In fact, weekend brunch, served on white wrought-iron tables on the columned and covered front porch, is popular with city residents and overnight guests alike.

Located two blocks from Santa Fe's famous plaza, Grant Corner Inn is operated by longtime innkeeper Louise Stewart. Louise, whose father founded the Camelback Inn in Scottsdale, is an interior designer.

The proprietor also operates the Grant Corner Inn Hacienda, a Southwestern-style condo with two guest rooms, each offered in the low $100 range. The Hacienda is located about five blocks from the inn.

ROOMS FOR ROMANCE

Of the inn's dozen accommodations, we recommend Rooms 3, 7, 8, and 10 for romantic getaways. Often booked far in advance, Room 8 (mid $100 range), a second-floor hideaway that faces the front of the property, is the most popular. Decorated in navy and white with lace curtains, the room holds a king-sized brass and iron bed, an Austrian ceramic stove reproduction, and an antique love seat. The bathroom has a shower stall. Guests here share the balcony with Room 7 (mid $100 range), located next door.

Room 7 is the only accommodation featuring Southwestern decor. The centerpiece is a grand, king-sized pencil-post bed made of pine. Indian rugs cover the floor, and the bathroom has a clawfoot tub-and-shower combination.

Located high on the third floor, the very private Room 10 (low to mid $100 range) has mauve-colored walls, a queen-sized bed, and a sitting area with a love seat.

Room 3 (mid $100 range) occupies a rear corner on the second floor and is appointed with an antique German armoire, a queen-sized, iron four-poster bed, and an in-room antique sink. The tiled bathroom has a clawfoot tub-and-shower combination.

Rooms 5 and 6 share a bathroom. The bathroom for Room 11 is across the hall.

x

İ n n ᴏ ꜰ ᴛ ʜ ᴇ Ꭺ ɴ ᴀ ꜱ ᴀ ᴢ ɪ

113 Washington Avenue

Santa Fe, NM 87501

Telephone toll free: (800) 688-8100

Fifty-nine rooms, each with private bath and gas fireplace. Restaurant. Handicapped access. Smoking is
allowed. Four-night minimum stay required during
holiday periods. Deluxe.

Getting There

From Albuquerque, drive north on Interstate 25, and
exit at St. Francis Drive/Highway 285, and follow
north to the second Paseo de Peralta exit. Turn right
and follow into downtown Santa Fe. Turn right on
Washington Avenue and follow to inn on left.

Those who have spent any time in the Southwest are aware of the tendency among some interior designers to overdose on generic or clichéd regional decor, from cactus lamps to log furnishings.

At Inn of the Anasazi (*Anasazi* is Navajo for "the ancient ones"), the perfect balance has been struck. You won't be overwhelmed by Southwestern kitsch, but neither will there be any doubt about where you are.

One of Santa Fe's newest and most special places to stay, this small hotel is understated and elegant. The style isn't fussy, yet the feeling is rich, textured, and inviting. It also enjoys a perfect location for shoppers and downtown explorers: just steps from the historic plaza. Without a doubt, this is *the* place to stay in Santa Fe. It's also one of the most expensive.

ROOMS FOR ROMANCE

Accommodations consist of deluxe rooms (around $400), superior king rooms (mid $200 range), and somewhat small standard rooms with king-sized beds (low to mid $200 range). From November through March rates are lower. Parking costs around $10 per day, and breakfast is not included.

All of the inn's guest rooms are subtly yet comfortably styled. Walls are hand-plastered, pine floors are covered with handsome rugs, and ceilings, themselves works of art, boast traditional *vigas* inlaid with patterned *latillas*. Windows are shuttered, and light is provided by attractive lamps, some fashioned from twisted wrought iron. Four-poster iron beds and gas-lit, kiva-style fireplaces complement the romantic ambience.

Amenities include cotton sheets, towels, and robes; stereo cassette players; televisions with videocassette players (movie tapes may be ordered from your room); and twice-daily maid service. You can even have an exercise bike brought to your door.

Adobe Pines Inn
Highway 68
Ranchos de Taos, NM 87557
Telephone toll free: (800) 723-8267

Five rooms, each with private bath and woodburning kiva fireplace; two with tubs for two. Complimentary full breakfast served at tables for two. No handicapped access. Smoking is not permitted indoors. Two-night minimum stay required during weekends; four-night minimum during holiday periods. Moderate to expensive.

Getting There
The inn is located approximately four miles south of Taos and a half mile south of the Historic Ranchos Plaza just off the east side of Highway 68.

In anticipation of reaching the historic downtown area, most Taos-bound couples heading north along Highway 68 are probably completely unaware that one of New Mexico's most romantic inns sits just off the road, less than ten minutes from town. This somewhat hidden location only contributes to the allure of Adobe Pines Inn, among our most prized Southwestern discoveries.

Guests reach the 150-year-old adobe home-turned-inn by crossing a footbridge over a creek. The structure is fronted by a grassy courtyard and a grand portal with a stone floor and beamed ceiling. Comfortable chairs are placed along its eighty-foot expanse.

Innkeepers Chuck and Charil Fulkerson labored for months to convert the property to an inn, but they were careful to preserve the antique charm and authentic detailing. Visitors will appreciate the improvements made by the couple, including the modern bathrooms.

Rooms for Romance

Adobe Pines Inn holds two of the Southwest's most romantic rooms: Puerta Rosa and Puerta Violetta. Puerta Rosa (mid $100 range), which has a *viga* ceiling and polished brick floor, is appointed with antiques and a corner kiva fireplace.

The queen-sized bed has a wrought-iron headboard. The most romantic feature, however, is five steps down from the bedroom, where a grand bathroom awaits. This slice of heaven, which comes complete with bubbles and candles, has wide pine floors and a *viga* ceiling, its own kiva fireplace, a sitting area, tiled double sinks, a tiled soaking tub for two, a tiled shower stall, and a sauna for two.

Puerta Violetta (mid $100 range), created in the early 1990s, is the inn's only second-floor guest room, and it offers a private roof deck. A queen-sized iron bed sits on a carpeted floor before a corner kiva fireplace. A couple of steps up from the bedroom is a beautiful tiled bath with an oval spa tub for two under a treetop window. There's also a separate shower stall. This room has a view of Taos Mountain.

The innkeepers recently added two spacious new suites (mid $100 range) that each offer French doors, a gas fireplace, a fountain, and a bathroom complete with a spa tub for two, a tiled shower, and another gas fireplace.

Located off the main portal, Puerta Azul is the inn's smallest room, offered at the time of our visit for around $100. This intriguing hideaway, with a queen-sized bed, kiva fireplace, and mustard-colored plaster walls, exudes an almost spiritual ambience. Puerta Verde (around $100) has a small bathroom that's not completely private.

CASA DE LAS CHIMENEAS
BED & BREAKFAST INN
405 Cordoba Road
Taos, NM 87571
Telephone: (505) 758-4777

Four rooms, each with private bath, kiva fireplace, refrigerators with complimentary drinks, and television. Complimentary full breakfast served in your room. Hot tub. No handicapped access. Smoking is not permitted. No minimum stay requirement. Moderate to expensive.

Getting There
From Highway 68 just south of Taos's historic downtown center, turn east on Los Pandos Road. Drive one block to Cordoba Road (four-way stop) and turn right. Inn is on the left.

CASA DE LAS CHIMENEAS
BED & BREAKFAST INN ❖ *Taos*

Thumb through the pages of this book and you'll notice that we tend to eschew the three- and four-room B&Bs that seem to have proliferated in recent years, not just in the Southwest but throughout the nation. In our travels, we've unfortunately visited too many small inns where the hosts were overbearing or unseasoned, and where we felt like uncomfortable strangers in someone else's home.

We have no such misgivings about recommending Casa de las Chimeneas, the proverbial small package in which good things really do come. At this petite hideaway, you'll be welcomed by skilled innkeepers who won't smother you with their presence, and you'll immediately feel comfortable and cozy in your room. Each room, by the way, has its own private outdoor entry.

Hidden behind seven-foot-tall adobe walls in a well-tended neighborhood less than three blocks from Taos Plaza, the inn is named for the many chimneys that warm its interior. The setting is lovely, with expansive gardens that burst with colorful flowers from spring through fall. Cottonwood trees sway gently above an outdoor hot tub on the inn's back patio.

ROOMS FOR ROMANCE

Offered in the mid $100 range, the Library Suite is the most expensive of the inn's four rooms. It includes a sitting room with a beamed ceiling and wood floor, built-in bookshelves, a sofa sleeper, a kiva fireplace, and a game table. One step down is the bedroom in which a queen-sized bed sits on brick floors. There's another kiva fireplace here, as well as an antique writing desk. An attractive bathroom with a tub-and-shower combination looks out on a rear garden area.

The newest room, Garden (low to mid $100 range), has pine floors, a handsome wood ceiling, a kiva fireplace, a sitting area under a skylight, and a king-sized bed with a hand-carved headboard. Another skylight illuminates the shower and deep soaking tub for one.

The Willow Room (low $100 range) is appointed with *equipale* chairs and a king-sized bed. A kiva fireplace sits in a corner. The bathroom holds a large tiled shower.

The centerpiece of the Blue Room (low $100 range) is an attractive kiva fireplace, which is visible from the king-sized bed. There's a tub-and-shower combination and an unusual mirror with intricate tin work in the custom-tiled bathroom.

CASA EUROPA
157 Upper Ranchitos Road
Taos, NM 87571
Telephone: (505) 758-9798

Seven rooms, each with private bath; six with fireplaces.
Complimentary full breakfast served at communal table.
Hot tub and sauna. No handicapped access. Smoking
is not permitted. Two-night minimum stay during week-
ends; three- to five-night minimum during holiday periods.
Moderate.

Getting There
From Highway 68 in Ranchos de Taos, turn west on
Highway 240/Lower Ranchitos Road and follow past
Martinez Hacienda. Turn left on Upper Ranchitos
Road and follow to inn on left.

CASA EUROPA ❖ *Taos*

On the lookout for what had been described as a two-century-old adobe, we passed right by Casa Europa the first time, mistaking the inn's contemporary-style and multiwindowed façade for that of a newer private home. We discovered later that the owners worked for six years to transform the structure into Casa Europa, adding more than a dozen skylights and scores of windows in the process.

The expanse of glass not only creates a warm and romantic ambience, it showcases an appealing and restful country setting that sets Casa Europa apart from most of our other Taos destinations. It's refreshingly quiet and peaceful out here, yet the town plaza is only a two-minute drive away.

ROOMS FOR ROMANCE

Situated off the center courtyard and accessed through a sliding door, the Spa Room (low $100 range) is a house favorite. A king-sized bed sits on a heated *saltillo* tiled floor near a kiva fireplace. Adjacent to the bed, behind an antique Mexican wooden screen, sits a sunken spa tub for two. The bathroom contains a shower that doubles as a steam sauna.

The Suite (mid $100 range), the inn's newest room, was at one time a private residence. Consequently, it's fully equipped with a kitchen and dining area; a living room with a Taos sofa, a kiva fireplace, and a *banco*; and a bedroom with a queen-sized bed. A separate brick-floored room holds a two-person spa.

In the French Room (around $100), a striking, century-old brass queen-sized bed from France is centered on a hand-hewn wood floor that's also over a hundred years old. Above is a beautiful, white, coved *viga* ceiling. A kiva fireplace is visible from the bed. The marble bathroom has a shower, and French doors open onto a courtyard.

The Southwest Room (around $100) is a large second-floor hideaway with views of the surrounding mountains. A king-sized bed sits in a cozy, curtained alcove adjacent to a sitting room with a porcelain wood stove, a love seat, a chair, and a writing desk. The room is carpeted and features a dark *viga* ceiling. The white marble bathroom has a spa-tub-and-shower combination.

A little wooden structure on the property houses a communal hot tub and a Swedish sauna.

Old Taos Guesthouse

1028 Witt Road

Taos, NM 87571

Telephone: (505) 758-5448; toll-free: (800) 758-5448

Eight rooms, each with private bath; five with fireplaces. Complimentary continental breakfast served at tables for two and four or in your room. No handicapped access. Smoking is not permitted. Two-night minimum stay required during some weekends; three-night minimum during holiday periods. Moderate.

Getting There

From northbound Highway 68 in downtown Taos, turn east on Kit Carson Road and follow to Witt Road. Turn right and follow to inn on right.

Visit the historic Kit Carson home in Taos and you'll get a taste of what life might have been like here in the mid 1800s. It was during this period in Taos's romantic history that a trapper built a little adobe at the base of the mountains, just up the road from the home of Kit and his new bride Josefa.

In the late 1980s, the little hacienda, which had been expanded from time to time over the years, was renovated by ski enthusiasts Tim and Leslie Reeves, who transformed it into an exceptional inn. The couple has achieved that perfect balance between historic authenticity and contemporary romantic comforts.

Located just under two miles from the Taos Plaza in the Cañon neighborhood, the seven-acre property offers sweeping views of Taos Valley. Three earth-colored wings face a small courtyard lawn, and Adirondack-style chairs sit outside guest room doors under beamed verandas.

Rooms for Romance

At Old Taos Guesthouse we discovered two of the most romantic rooms in all of Taos: the Sunset Suite and the Taos Suite. The Sunset Suite (around $100) is a spacious carpeted hideaway with a step-up sitting area where two Taos-style chairs face a gas kiva fireplace that's flanked by small *bancos*. The king-sized Taos-style bed sits under a ceiling with *vigas* and *latillas,* and the pueblo-style bathroom has a shower stall.

Offered for just a few dollars more is the Taos Suite, which features hardwood floors, a full kitchen, a *viga* ceiling, a couch, and two pigskin chairs. A *banco* that juts from the enchanting woodburning kiva fireplace separates the bed area from the sitting room. The king-sized bed is placed on a two-step platform under a large window overlooking trees and lawn. A cozy bathroom with wall murals holds a clawfoot tub.

Room 7 (under $100) faces the backyard and boasts an eighty-mile vista of Taos Valley as well as a view of wonderful sunsets. This hundred-year-old room has hardwood floors, a *viga* ceiling, and thick adobe walls. The bathroom has a shower and a hand-painted tile sink, one of several pieces designed by innkeeper Tim.

Room 5 (under $100) is a private corner room in which a queen-sized bed is placed under an octagonal window and a painted beam ceiling. The bathroom has a cozy tub in a redwood frame.

La Posada de Taos

309 Juanita Lane
Taos, NM 87571
Telephone: (505) 758-8164

Six rooms, each with private bath. Complimentary full breakfast served at a communal table. No handicapped access. Smoking is not permitted. Two-night minimum stay required during weekends; three-night minimum during holiday periods. Moderate.

Getting There
From Highway 68, called Paseo del Pueblo Sur in Taos, turn west into plaza and drive straight onto Don Fernando. Drive two blocks, turn left on Manzanares, and turn right on Juanita Lane. Follow to inn on right.

LA POSADA DE TAOS ❖ *Taos*

Taos may be one of the Southwest's most popular destinations, but don't assume that a weekend here will necessarily drain your bank account. At this historic adobe, located in a quiet neighborhood just two blocks from Taos Plaza, we discovered some of the region's most moderately priced romantic rooms. In fact, La Posada de Taos just might be the Southwest's best romantic value.

Reportedly the first B&B in Taos, the inn passed to new owners Bill and Nancy Swan in 1993; they fell in love with the place during a visit from their home in northern Virginia. Since their arrival, the innkeepers have created a sixth room and have made a number of improvements.

ROOMS FOR ROMANCE

Offered at the time of our visit for around $100, La Casa de la Luna de Miel (the Honeymoon House) is a bargain-priced hideaway for romantics. This freestanding love nest is situated within the walls of the inn's property but is about thirty feet from the inn's front door—plenty of space to ensure privacy. Inside, a three-step ladder leads to a cozy double bed set in a skylit loft from which you'll be able to see the stars. There's also a sitting area with a kiva fireplace and a private walled courtyard.

The inn's newest accommodation, El Solecito (low $100 range), is a split-level room with brick and tile floors. A lovely queen-sized bed sits on the raised upper level, above a sitting room with two willow chairs and a large kiva fireplace. Antique Mexican doors open onto a private patio, and the two-level tiled bathroom has a spa tub under a skylight.

Beutler (low $100 range), the largest room in the house, has a private entrance, a king-sized bed, a chaise longue, a game table, a window seat, and a woodburning stove. The nice bathroom contains a Southwestern-style adobe shower stall and a spa tub into which the two of you might be able to squeeze.

The Liño Room holds a two-hundred-year-old Dutch pine bed (queen-sized), a woodburning stove, a handsome English church pew, and an antique Mexican armoire. The tiny bathroom contains a shower stall and an antique washstand.

The Monterey Room (around $100) is a small and cozy room in the oldest part of the house. It has a private entrance and is equipped with a kiva fireplace, a queen-sized bed, a sitting area, and a tiny bathroom with a shower stall.

The smallest room is called Taos (less than $100), and has a small bathroom with a tub-and-shower combination, a small sitting area, and a view of Taos Mountain.

Taos Hacienda Inn
102 La Loma Plaza
Taos, NM 87571
Telephone: (505) 758-1717

Seven rooms, each with private bath and fireplace. Complimentary full breakfast served at tables for two and four. In-ground spa. No handicapped access. Smoking is not permitted. Two-night minimum stay required during weekends; Three- to six-night minimum during holiday periods. Moderate to expensive.

Getting There
From northbound Highway 68 in Taos, just south of Holy Cross Hospital, turn west on La Posta Road and follow to Ranchitos Road. Turn right and follow to inn on left, at the corner of Ranchitos Road and Valdez Lane.

You could spend a week in Taos without stumbling upon this delightful upscale inn set on a gentle tree-shaded hill a scant three blocks from the plaza. Hidden behind two-hundred-year-old walls with minimal signage, the inn overlooks Taos and the Sangre de Cristo Range, as well as Taos Mountain.

Since emerging from a spare-no-expense renovation in the early 1990s, Taos Hacienda Inn has earned a reputation as the community's poshest B&B, but those in the know guard it as a secret. It's our personal Taos favorite.

With its graceful balconies, covered and beamed porches, patios, and warming kivas, this resplendent pueblo-style structure oozes Southwestern romance. Public rooms are warm and inviting, and guest quarters feature updated appointments and fresh flowers. Thick interior walls add charm as well as privacy.

At the time of our visit, husband and wife innkeepers Jerry Davis and Peggy Osterfoss, the creators of this romantic haven, were dividing their time between Taos and Colorado, where both were active in civic affairs. Peggy is a former mayor of Vail and Jerry held the mayor's post in Avon.

ROOMS FOR ROMANCE

The inn's most decadent accommodation is Carey's Studio (upper $100 range), a second-floor guest house suite that's tucked behind a Dutch-style door under the branches of an old elm tree. Windows on three walls provide nice vistas of the distant mountains.

Named for local artist Carey Moore, who once painted here, the suite is spacious and luxurious, featuring wool carpeting, a fireplace, a couch, and a trundle bed placed against a wall of windows. A carved wooden screen separates the sitting room from the bed area, whose centerpiece is a king-sized bed with a pine headboard carved with a sunburst. There's also a kitchenette and a private outdoor sitting area. The bathroom has a tiled tub-and-shower combination.

La Loma (mid to upper $100 range) is a relatively new room with a private outdoor entrance, a kitchenette, and a pine-floored sitting room equipped with a couch, a kiva fireplace, and a table and chairs. The step-up bed landing holds a king-sized bed embellished with decorative tin. Guests here also have a tiny private patio.

A rocking horse and Old West knickknacks adorn Happy Trails (low to mid $100 range), which has windows on three sides, a fireplace with a tiled hearth, and a queen-sized brass bed. French doors provide access to a private outdoor sitting area. The contemporary but tiny bathroom is outfitted with a tiled tub-and-shower combination.

For the economy minded, Wildrose (around $100) is a cozy hideaway on the second floor with sponge-painted walls, *latilla* shutters, and a *latilla*-style headboard on the queen-sized bed. The step-up tiled bathroom contains a tub-and-shower combination.

HACIENDA DEL SOL
Highway 64
Taos, NM 87571
Telephone: (505) 758-0287

Nine rooms, each with private bath; eight with fireplaces. Complimentary full breakfast served at tables
for four or six. Hot tub. Limited handicapped access.
Smoking is not permitted. Two-night minimum stay
required during weekends; three-night minimum
during holiday periods. Moderate.

Getting There
From downtown Taos, follow Highway 68 north,
which veers left and becomes Highway 64. One mile
north of the Taos Inn, watch for the inn's sign and
gravel road on the right. Follow the gravel road past
large rocks to inn on left.

On a warm summer night, listen closely and you may hear drums from nearby Taos Pueblo. Soak in the outdoor hot tub and you might be treated to a dance of lightning over distant Taos Mountain. At Hacienda del Sol, the pueblo dwellers are your neighbors and Taos Mountain, as the innkeepers say, "is our backyard."

One of Taos's most historic properties, the inn was once part of the estate of the late Mabel Dodge Luhan, a well-known Taos art patroness whose houseguests included Georgia O'Keeffe and D. H. Lawrence.

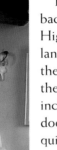

The rambling, tree-shaded estate, set back a comfortable distance off of Highway 64 and abutting open Indian lands, consists of three adobe buildings, the oldest of which was constructed in the early 1800s. Traditional touches here include *viga* ceilings with *latillas*, arched doorways, and thick adobe walls. Pretty quilts adorn every bed.

ROOMS FOR ROMANCE

The inn's rooms are each equipped with a cassette player and Indian flute tapes. All but one have fireplaces.

Los Amantes (low $100 range), a sumptuous suite in the main house, features a private patio entry via French doors. A picture window overlooks a shaded lawn area, and the beautiful ceiling features pine *vigas* and Aspen *latillas*. A huge spa tub for two sits in a mahogany frame in a separate room under a *viga* ceiling and skylight. The bathroom contains a tub-and-shower combination.

Among some newer rooms added in the mid 1990s is the Taos Suite (low $100 range), equipped with a queen-sized iron bed, two rocking chairs facing a gas fireplace, and a large bathroom with a skylit spa tub for two.

Furnished with Southwestern collectibles, two *equipale* chairs, and a Taos drum table, the Adobe Room (around $100) is another romantic choice. This charmer also has a kiva fireplace and a *viga* and *latilla* ceiling. You'll step up to a sunny bathroom with double sinks and a shower that also functions as a steam room.

The most remote hideaway is Rio Grande (around $100), a newer room outfitted with a queen-sized sleigh bed of dark wood and two Taos-style chairs, which are set before a kiva fireplace. The floor is of polished tile, and the windows are shuttered with red willow. French doors open to a rear lawn and patio area.

SALSA DEL SALTO
Taos Ski Valley Road
Taos, NM
Telephone: (505) 776-2422

Eight rooms, each with private bath. Complimentary
full breakfast served at communal table. Swimming
pool, spa, and two tennis courts. Handicapped access.
Smoking is allowed outdoors only. No minimum stay
requirement. Moderate to expensive.

Getting There
From downtown Taos, follow Highway 68/Paseo del
Pueblo Norte north out of town. The road becomes
Highway 522 north of Taos. Five miles north of Taos
Plaza, turn right on Highway 150/Taos Ski Valley
Road and follow five miles to inn on right.

SALSA DEL SALTO ✦ *Taos*

I f your daytime destination is Taos Ski Valley, but your dinner reservations are waiting in Taos, you'll welcome a romantic middle ground at the base of the Sangre de Cristo Mountains. From your cozy nest at Salsa del Salto, you can reach the ski slopes in about fifteen minutes; drive about ten miles in the other direction and you'll be browsing the shops around Taos Plaza before dining.

Converted from a stylish private residence into an equally luxurious small inn a few years ago by French-born ski champion and hotelier Dadou Mayer and his wife, Mary Hocket, Salsa del Salto is a stunning country estate that's warm, friendly, and informal.

In the living room, guests often gather before the soaring rock fireplace for conversation and snacks, including chips and salsa, of course. Nearby, a refrigerator full of complimentary refreshments is available around the clock. Outside there's a nice swimming pool (open during summer), a spa (heated year round), and two tennis courts. Wide open spaces surround the property.

ROOMS FOR ROMANCE

Each of the inn's eight king-bedded rooms promises romantic potential, but there's no argument about which accommodation is the best. The Master's Suite (high $100 range) on the second floor is the preeminent honeymoon hideaway. This large skylit retreat has a fireplace gilded with brass, a cathedral ceiling, and a huge bathroom with a tiled spa tub for two, a separate shower, double sinks, and a bidet. This room also has a private balcony and two entrances.

For privacy seekers, we recommend the Lobo and Kachina rooms (around $100), which are located in an adjacent guest house. These wool-carpeted units have *viga* ceilings, mountain-view windows, and bathrooms that are equipped with tub-and-shower combinations.

The corner window in Antoine's Room (low $100 range) affords views of Taos Mountain and the Tuchas peaks. Sunset lovers will enjoy the west-facing Taos Mesa Room (low $100 range).

CHALET MONTESANO
1 Pattison Loop Road
Taos Ski Valley, NM 87525
Telephone: (505) 776-8226

Seven rooms and suites, each with private bath; four
with woodburning fireplaces. Indoor swimming pool
and spa. No handicapped access. Smoking is allowed.
Two-night minimum stay required during weekends;
four-night minimum during holiday periods.
Moderate to deluxe.

Getting There
From downtown Taos, follow Highway 68/Paseo del
Pueblo Norte north out of town. The road becomes
Highway 522 north of Taos. Five miles north of Taos
Plaza, turn right on Highway 150/Taos Ski Valley
Road and follow to Taos Ski Valley. At the resort,
follow the road as it loops around the large parking
area and right onto Thining Road. Turn right on
Pattison Loop Road and follow to inn.

CHALET MONTESANO ❖ *Taos Ski Valley*

U nlike many charmless resort area accommodations we've visited that seem to exist solely
for the purpose of providing a few hours of sleep for skiers, Chalet Montesano is a breath
of fresh mountain air. In fact, this alpine gem is so inviting and comfortable, serious skiers should
beware. With romantic guest rooms and great fitness facilities under one roof, you may be tempted
to abandon the slopes altogether.

Hidden away among the pines above the busy Taos Ski Valley village center, this former private
residence is within easy walking distance to the lifts. In the warmer months, visitors will find the
inn a convenient base for day hikes and mountain bike excursions.

Skiers are provided with conveniences such as ski packages, a ski boot dryer, and a clothes
washer and dryer. Nonskiers can work out in a well-equipped exercise room or in the indoor
lap pool, both of which are enclosed in glass.
There's also a spa for those après-ski evenings
and summer nights.

ROOMS FOR ROMANCE
Room 9 (mid $200 range), the inn's most
impressive and largest accommodation, has
a king-sized bed and attractive furnishings
crafted from redwood and cedar. There's
also a full kitchen and private balcony.

Room 6 (mid $100 range) is a minisuite high
on the third floor. This spacious hideaway is
equipped with a queen-sized, European-style
carved bed and matching furniture, including
a table and chairs. There's a forest view from
small corner windows. The bathroom has a
tub-and-shower combination.

Rooms 7 and 8 (low $200 range) are classified as studio apartments. These six-hundred-square-
foot units have full kitchens, fireplaces, dining and living rooms, queen-sized Murphy beds, and
bathrooms with tub-and-shower combinations. Rooms 7 and 8 share a mountain-view deck.

Our least favorite suites are 1 and 3, which are located on the inn's ground floor and are not
as bright and cheery as those on the higher levels.

All rooms are equipped with televisions, telephones, and audio systems. Children over age
fourteen are welcome. Rates noted above are for winter. Summer tariffs are considerably less.

SOUTHWESTERN COLORADO

Daytime Diversions

The magnificent cliff dwellings of the Anasazi Indians are preserved at Mesa Verde National Park, southeast of Cortez. One of the structures, Cliff Palace, is the largest of its kind in the world.

The Durango-Silverton Narrow Gauge Railroad operates very popular forty-five-mile excursions through the mountains between charming Durango and the historic burg of Silverton.

Adventurous visitors can raft the Animas River or rent a four-wheel-drive vehicle and visit remote Alta, a mountain ghost town located about thirty minutes outside Durango.

During the warmer months, the Purgatory-Durango ski resort, twenty-five miles north of Durango, offers alpine slide and chairlift rides, mountain biking trails, and music concerts.

The route along Highways 145 and 160 from Mancos and Cortez to Telluride is part of the San Juan Skyway scenic route, affording vistas ranging from red rock formations to fourteen-thousand-foot-high snowy peaks.

At Great Sand Dunes Country Club and Inn, mountain bikes as well as horses can be rented.

Tables for Two

Great Sand Dunes Country Club and Inn, Mosca (described in this section)
Millwood Junction, Highways 160/184, Mancos
Old Germany, Highway 145, Dolores
Ariano's Restaurant, 160 East Sixth Street, Durango
Randy's, 152 East Sixth Street, Durango
Palace Grill, One Depot Place, Durango

GREAT SAND DUNES
COUNTRY CLUB AND INN
5303 Highway 150
Mosca, CO 81146
Telephone toll-free: (800) 284-9213

Fifteen rooms, each with private bath. Complimentary
full breakfast served in the ranch's restaurant. Restaurant,
golf course, swimming pool, sauna, spa, and fitness
center. Handicapped access. Smoking is not permitted.
Two-night minimum stay required during weekends.
Closed January. Expensive to deluxe.

Getting There
From the east or west, follow Highway 160 to
Highway 150 and drive north twelve miles to resort.
From the north or south via Highway 17, follow
County Lane 6 for sixteen miles east. Turn south
on Highway 150 and follow south one mile to resort.

GREAT SAND DUNES
COUNTRY CLUB AND INN ❖ *Mosca*

I f one were to craft a short list of the Southwest's natural wonders, the Great Sand Dunes National Monument would certainly be worthy of a spot. This fifty-seven-square-mile desert, with towering dunes set incongruously among the craggy Rockies, provides a heavenly setting for one of our most unusual romantic getaways. It's especially recommended for those seeking a change from the region's more mainstream destinations like Telluride, Taos, and Santa Fe.

The Great Sand Dunes Country Club and Inn occupies land once known as the Zapata and Medano Ranches. Former New York City architect Hisayoshi (Hisa) Ota bought some one

hundred thousand acres a few years ago and carved out a luscious spread that now includes a championship eighteen-hole golf course and a collection of restored buildings, including a former stagecoach stop, a blacksmith's shop, and a horse barn.

Much of the handmade furniture in the rooms was crafted by Berle Lewis, the ranch's longtime handyman, who achieved worldwide notoriety in the 1960s. One of Berle's horses was the first of several animals mysteriously killed by what he and many others believed were aliens from UFOs.

High season at the inn is July through late September; off-season rates are considerably lower. Golf packages are available.

ROOMS FOR ROMANCE

Rooms at the inn don't contain televisions or telephones, and there are no newspapers sold on the property. Guest rooms are appointed simply with custom furnishings and luscious quilts, reflecting a country and Southwestern theme. Many rooms have gorgeous views of the desert, the dunes, and the distant mountains.

Another of the ranch's historic structures is an antique bunkhouse that today holds five of the inn's guest rooms. All of these log-walled units have clawfoot tubs and pedestal sinks. Among the most frequently requested is Room 9 (mid $200 range) in the bunkhouse; it's actually a suite that includes a sitting room and a woodburning stove.

Ota's favorite is Room 5 (high $100 range) in the inn building because of its loft effect and great view.

LOGWOOD

35060 Highway 550 North
Durango, CO 81301
Telephone: (303) 259-4396

Six rooms, each with private bath. Complimentary
full breakfast served at a communal table or in your
room (for an extra charge). Complimentary evening
dessert. No handicapped access. Smoking is not permitted. Two-night minimum stay required during
weekends and holiday periods; three-night minimum
during Christmas holidays. Moderate.

Getting There
From Highway 160 in Durango, drive north through
town on Highway 550 for approximately twelve miles
to the blue lodging sign on right. Turn right past the
mail boxes, then take an immediate right into the
inn's driveway. If you pass the KOA campground
on Highway 550, you've gone too far north.

Entering Durango from the south, we frankly wondered whether the community would prove to be a suitably romantic destination. The hills were sunburned and barren, and charmless buildings lined the highway.

Our impression improved as we drove through the busy, well-preserved downtown, and by the time we reached the green and woodsy northern outskirts of town we were completely smitten.

Logwood, an enchanting, two-story, log-walled structure about twelve miles north of Durango, takes full advantage of the beautiful Animas River valley. The inn is surrounded by trees and cuddles right up to the river. A large deck overlooks the hillside and rushing water. Deer and beaver can often be seen on the property.

ROOMS FOR ROMANCE

At the time of our visit, almost all the rooms were being offered for less than $100 per night during the high-season summer months. Winter rates were between $50 and $100, making Logwood an all-season romantic bargain.

Guest rooms and bathrooms are comparatively small, but each is equipped with the essentials. They all have large windows to take advantage of the glorious outdoors, and the beds are covered with hand-stitched quilts.

One of the nicest rooms is Mesa Verde, a second-floor hideaway done in rose, yellow, and blue. The room has a queen-sized bed and offers a river view. The bathroom has a tub-and-shower combination.

In the Animas Suite (low $100 range) on the lower level, French doors connect the sitting room and bedroom. The sitting room contains a couch, a television, and a videocassette player, as well as a gas stove that can be seen from the bedroom.

A view of a rugged cliff and the surrounding woods awaits from the Fawn Room, while the Durango Room, a rear second-floor corner, faces the branches of a majestic oak tree.

Aspen, the inn's smallest room, has a double bed.

Lightner Creek Inn
Bed and Breakfast
999 County Road 207
Durango, CO 81301
Telephone: (303) 259-1226

Eight rooms, six with private baths. Complimentary full breakfast served at communal table or tables for two. Handicapped access. Smoking is not permitted. Two-night minimum stay preferred during holiday periods. Moderate to expensive.

Getting There
From Durango, drive west on Highway 160 for three miles, and turn right on County Road 207. Follow for one mile to inn on left.

Lightner Creek Inn
Bed and Breakfast ❖ *Durango*

One of our most enjoyable tasks is touring the city streets, neighborhoods, and back roads of various communities and narrowing down long lists of local inns to the most romantic. We discovered the standard bearer of Durango in lovely Lightner Creek Canyon about four miles from town.

The canyon's namesake inn occupies a pastoral, twenty-acre parcel that includes llama and horse pastures, manicured lawns and gardens, a duck pond, and stands of tall trees. Bald eagles, wild turkeys, and falcons are among the inhabitants of an adjacent wildlife refuge.

The inn itself is an attractive turn-of-the-century cottage and freestanding carriage house, which has been enlarged and remodeled with apparent great care over the years. Furnishings are of high quality, and the public and guest rooms are tastefully papered and nicely windowed.

Rooms for Romance

Our favorite room is found on the second level of the carriage house, located a few steps from the main inn. The seven-hundred-square-foot suite (mid $100 range) affords a view of aspen trees and the nearby mountainside. The room is furnished with a fluffy king-sized bed, an oak table and chairs placed under a set of windows, comfortable chairs, and a pellet stove. French doors open onto a small deck. The spacious bathroom holds a large tiled shower that's big enough for the two of you.

In the main house, the most popular room among visiting romantics is Karen Olivia (around $100), a second-floor rear corner room in which a beautiful queen-sized pine bed covered in white Battenburg linens is placed diagonally. This room offers a view of the backyard, the gazebo, the creek, and the wooded mountainside. A honeymoon package with romantic amenities is available for this and other rooms for about $50 more.

The Vicki Lynn and Svea Elen rooms (around $100) both have private entrances via French doors from a brick patio. Both of these rooms have queen-sized beds.

Romantic travelers should note that the Kimberly Jane and Eleanor Lucy rooms share a bathroom.

BLUE LAKE RANCH
16919 Highway 140
Hesperus, CO 81326
Telephone: (303) 385-4537

Nine rooms and cottages, each with private bath.
Complimentary full breakfast buffet served in dining
room. Limited handicapped access. Smoking is
not permitted. Two-night minimum stay required.
Moderate to deluxe.

Getting There
From Durango, follow Highway 160 west for eleven
miles to Hesperus. Turn south on Highway 140 and
drive for six and a half miles (use your odometer) to
gravel drive on the right. (The drive is 1.3 miles north
of the Highway 141 junction.) Follow the gravel
drive to inn.

BLUE LAKE RANCH ❖ *Hesperus*

To describe Blue Lake Ranch as an inn would be both a disservice and an understatement. It's more like a small romantic community, a utopia for lovers in which the population rarely exceeds twenty. Easily one of the most romantic destinations in the western states, the ranch provides an array of intimate environments that should satisfy the most discriminating couples.

A collection of cozy, first-rate, bed-and-breakfast-style rooms and remote cottages, Blue Lake Ranch enjoys a very private mountain locale settled originally by a Swedish immigrant family. Innkeeper David Alford bought one hundred acres here in the late 1970s and set about renovating buildings and creating a comfortable retreat. During the renovation, he literally married the girl next door. Shirley, a physician, shares innkeeping duties. The couple also owns the Don Gaspar Compound in Santa Fe (see separate listing).

Rooms for Romance

Our personal favorite, the Cabin on the Lake (low to mid $200 range) is a three-bedroom, two-bath cottage set on the shore of private Blue Lake, in which guests have been known to dip sans swimsuits. Crafted from logs and stone, the cabin has a wraparound deck with rocking chairs. The romantic loft bedroom contains a stone fireplace and a king-sized bed and boasts mountain views to die for. Downstairs is a rock fireplace and comfy Taos furniture.

Cottage in the Woods (mid to upper $100 range) is reached via a wooded path from the main inn. Set amid a lush garden protected by deer fencing, the cottage has a kitchenette with *saltillo* tile and a bathroom with an oval spa tub for two. The step-up bedroom, with a king-sized bed, has cedar paneling and an open beam ceiling.

A little yellow homesteaders' cabin, now called River House (high $100), is nestled on the banks of La Plata River in a cottonwood grove. The living room is appointed with wicker furniture and it features a gas fireplace and television. There's also a *saltillo*-tiled kitchen. The bathroom holds a tub-and-shower combination, and one of the two bedrooms has a queen-sized bed.

In the main inn, the bright and sunny Garden Room (mid $100 range) has a fireplace, a chaise longue, and a love seat. The Blue Room (low $100 range), set under a dormer on the second floor, has a love seat and a mountain view. The private bathroom, which is placed at the foot of a private stairway, holds a deep soaking tub for two. We don't recommend the Victorian Room, whose bathroom is located across the hall.

Two comfortable suites (mid to upper $100 range) with living rooms and kitchens have been created in a former barn adjacent to the main inn. Both have king-sized beds, and one has a spa tub. Each has a private outdoor garden and sitting area.

LOST CANYON LAKE LODGE
15472 CR 35.3
Mancos, CO 81328
Telephone toll-free: (800) 992-1098

Five rooms, each with private bath. Complimentary full breakfast served at communal table, tables for two, or in your room. Hot tub. No handicapped access. Smoking is not permitted. Two-night minimum stay required during weekends and holiday periods. Moderate.

Getting There
From Highway 160 in Mancos, follow Highway 184 northwest for ten miles to inn sign on right. The inn is about forty miles from Durango and about twenty miles from the Mesa Verde cliff dwellings.

L O S T   C A N Y O N
L A K E   L O D G E   ❖   *Mancos*

Having worked as an intensive care nurse and an emergency department physician, respectively, Beth Newman and Ken Nickson are well suited to caring for folks. As Lost Canyon Lake Lodge's innkeepers, however, they're more apt to brew you a fresh pot of coffee or provide sightseeing tips than to provide bedside care.

One of the northernmost of our fifty destinations, Lost Canyon Lake Lodge perches on a hill near a pretty lake in the pines at a lofty elevation of over seven thousand feet. The two-story log structure has a covered wraparound porch and a scenic view deck overlooking a seemingly endless pine forest.

Also available to inn guests are a communal deck-mounted spa with a lake view, a hillside rock fire pit for cool mountain evenings, picnic tables, and hammocks.

Rooms for Romance

Both the Anasazi and Normandie rooms (around $100) have vaulted ceilings and soaring windows that overlook the lake and forest. These king-bedded rooms also have small sitting areas with chairs.

The Anasazi Room has handsome lodgepole pine furniture and a Southwestern theme, while the Normandie Room features a more delicate French country scheme with a carved rice bed.

The generously sized Homestead Room (under $100) contains a love seat, a queen-sized bed, and a romantic loft with another full-sized bed.

Mariah (under $100) overlooks the parking area, and Sundance (under $100) has twin beds.

More Travel Resources
for Incurable Romantics

Weekends for Two in Northern California: 50 Romantic Getaways (Second Edition)
More Weekends for Two in Northern California: 50 All-New Romantic Getaways
Weekends for Two in Southern California: 50 Romantic Getaways
Weekends for Two in the Pacific Northwest: 50 Romantic Getaways
Weekends for Two in New England: 50 Romantic Getaways

Each illustrated with more than 150 color photos, these books by Bill Gleeson are the definitive travel guides to the nation's most romantic destinations.

Free Travel Updates

We continue to discover new romantic destinations and reevaluate our currently featured inns and small hotels, and we're happy to share this information with readers. For a free update on our new discoveries and recommendations (and new books in the *Weekends for Two* series), please send a stamped, self-addressed business-sized envelope to Bill Gleeson, Weekends for Two Update, P.O. Box 6324, Folsom, CA 95763. We always appreciate hearing about your own romantic discoveries as well!

Cast Your Vote!
The Southwest's Most Romantic Hotel or Inn

Complete and mail to Bill Gleeson, Weekends for Two in the Southwest, P.O. Box 6324, Folsom, CA 95763. Enclose a self-addressed, stamped envelope for a free travel update.

Our favorite romantic retreat in the Southwest (does not have to be featured in this book):

_____
Name of hotel/inn

_____
City/Town (Arizona, New Mexico, or the Four Corners region)

What makes this place special:

_____

_____

Signed (addresses/names are not for publication):

_____
I have no connection with the operators of this property.

A Southwest Visitor's Glossary

If you're a first-time visitor to the Southwest, you'll likely hear or read a few unfamiliar words or see an unusual object or two. Following is a short glossary of terms that are somewhat unique to this romantic region.

banco: A pueblo-style seat, typically of plaster, built into a wall, often near a kiva. These often-cushioned places to snuggle were built with romantics in mind.

bultos: Wooden carvings of saints.

equipales: Mexican-style chairs and sofas whose seats and backs are constructed of stretched hide.

farolito: A paper bag with sand in the bottom in which a lighted candle is placed; called a *luminaria* south of Santa Fe.

kiva: A beehive-shaped fireplace found in the corners of many Southwestern guest rooms.

Kokopelli: The Native American flute player whose visage graces many Southwestern *objets d'art.*

latillas: Tightly spaced, rough-cut branches or strips of wood arranged as part of Southwest-style doors and shutter frames or between ceiling *vigas.*

luminaria: A paper bag with sand in the bottom in which a lighted candle is placed; called a *farolito* in the Santa Fe area.

nichos: Small recessed shelves in a wall or kiva fireplace where pottery and collectibles are displayed.

retablos: Paintings on wood of religious figures.

ristra: A hanging decorative cluster of dried peppers.

saguaro: This stately cactus with arms is pronounced saw-WAH-row.

Taos furniture: Taos furnishings referred to in this book are oversized, thick- and wide-cushioned chairs, sofas, and beds, often of log-frame construction. Some Taos sofas are large enough to also function as twin-sized beds.

vigas: These exposed log beams, often interspersed with plaster coving or with *latillas,* support the ceilings in many of the guest rooms described in this book.

vortex: A place of spiritual energy. The Sedona and Santa Fe regions, for example, are believed to have numerous vortices.

Index